The Celts

HUMAN BEHAVIOR
THE ART OF SEWING
THE OLD WEST
THE EMERGENCE OF MAN
THE AMERICAN WILDERNESS
THE TIME-LIFE ENCYCLOPEDIA OF GARDENING
LIFE LIBRARY OF PHOTOGRAPHY
THIS FABULOUS CENTURY
FOODS OF THE WORLD
TIME-LIFE LIBRARY OF AMERICA
TIME-LIFE LIBRARY OF ART
GREAT AGES OF MAN
LIFE SCIENCE LIBRARY
THE LIFE HISTORY OF THE UNITED STATES
TIME READING PROGRAM
LIFE NATURE LIBRARY
LIFE WORLD LIBRARY
FAMILY LIBRARY:
   THE TIME-LIFE BOOK OF THE FAMILY CAR
   THE TIME-LIFE FAMILY LEGAL GUIDE
   THE TIME-LIFE BOOK OF FAMILY FINANCE

The Emergence of Man

The Celts

by Duncan Norton-Taylor
and the Editors
of Time-Life Books

Time-Life Books
New York

The Author: DUNCAN NORTON-TAYLOR has served both as an editor for TIME and as managing editor of FORTUNE. His previous publications include a book about his experiences as a TIME correspondent in the South Pacific during World War II, entitled *With My Heart in My Mouth*. Norton-Taylor has been keenly interested in the Celts since he studied Irish literature at Brown University. He is currently preparing a biography of John Calvin.

The Consultants: Bruce D. Boling is Lecturer in English at the University of North Carolina, where he specializes in Irish history and literature. Bernard Wailes, Associate Professor of Anthropology at the University of Pennsylvania, has excavated ancient Celtic ruins in Ireland. Stuart Piggott is Abercromby Professor of Prehistoric Archeology at the University of Edinburgh, specializing in the archeology of the prehistoric peoples of Europe, particularly the Celts. Anne Ross, a former Senior Research Fellow at the University of Edinburgh, writes and lectures on Celtic life. Colonel John R. Elting, U.S.A. (Ret.), former Associate Professor of Military Art and Engineering at the United States Military Academy, is an authority on the history of warfare.

The Cover: A band of Celtic warriors in about 100 B.C. stands ready to do battle with another Celtic tribe in southern Britain. Characterized by the Greek writer Strabo as being "madly fond of war," the Celts were bellicose even among their own people. Each man armed himself according to his taste and wealth, usually with an iron-tipped spear—sometimes two to a man—and a large shield. In this painting by Michael A. Hampshire, the chieftain, wearing a checked woolen cloak, carries an elaborately decorated bronze shield while members of his band are poised grimly behind wooden ones reinforced and protected at the grip by a bronze boss.

Contents

Introduction

Even today, after more than a century of serious study, the popular conception of the Celts is crowded with erroneous stereotypes that span the entire range of their history: sinister Druids watching human sacrifices writhe, warriors rollicking in gore, charming but unreliable Irishmen, crusty and penurious Scots highlanders, hard and devious Welshmen. At best the present-day descendants of the Celts are widely viewed as clannish nationalists who are compulsively devoted to irrelevant and outmoded traditions. At worst the concepts of "Celtic" and "civilization" are never connected.

But the Celts did indeed develop a civilization, and it flourished not just in Ireland or on the British Isles, but first and most significantly in Continental Europe. In the period between 700 B.C. and 100 A.D. Celtic tribes thrived in France, Germany, Switzerland, Austria, Hungary and Czechoslovakia. During that span Celtic culture traversed the English Channel and the Irish Sea, and took root.

On the Continent Celtic culture—with its rigidly structured social organization, its religion administered by the Druids, its eloquent tradition of heroic legends passed down orally from generation to generation and its fantastic art—merged with Roman customs and traditions, sometimes losing its Celtic identity altogether. In England Celtic culture gave way to various aggressors: Romans, Angles, Saxons, Vikings, Normans.

Except for remote parts of Scotland and Wales, only Ireland remained a Celtic stronghold. Shielded by its surrounding waters from outside influences, Ireland preserved the Celtic traditions of rigidly organized tribal life, bardic poetry, vital "barbarian" art. Even the ancient language of Ireland's Celts —known popularly as Gaelic—persevered there.

No invaders, whether hostile or benevolent, could erase the Celtic imprint from Ireland. When Vikings raided the land and plundered its Celtic treasures, the Celtic creative spirit rebounded. When Christianity came to Ireland, it bent to Celtic ways; early Irish Christians would not be Romanized. In fact the Roman Church itself was to convey the ancient Celtic modes into modern life. Through the scholarly writings, the art and the poetry of Ireland's influential monks, elements of Celtic culture were even restored to the Continental homeland from which they had been driven.

Without the insights of the Celts drawn from the written records of medieval Irish monks, modern scholars would have to rely almost entirely on the writings of Classical Greek and Roman writers who, as conquerors, often deliberately misrepresented their adversaries. But many precious documents created by the Celts themselves have been preserved; archeology, too, furnishes indispensable clues. And perhaps the most vivid insight of all is provided by the people in parts of Ireland who still preserve many of the customs of the ancient Celts. By combining these elements, students of the past find it possible to reconstruct a true picture of these passionate, resourceful and creative people.

The Editors

Chapter One: A Passionate, Creative Breed

Once upon a time, according to an ancient Irish legend, in the province of Leinster there was a rich landholder named MacDatho who owned a famous hound. MacDatho's hound was known far and wide for its ability to run the 340 miles around the borders of Leinster in a single day. Ailill of Connaught and Conchobar of Ulster, rival monarchs, both sent messengers to MacDatho asking him for it. Unable to decide between the two demands without incurring the displeasure of either king, MacDatho invited both monarchs to a feast and produced from a cauldron an equally famous pig, fattened for seven years on the milk of 60 cows.

But who was going to carve it? The honor belonged to the greatest warrior present—that was the custom —and one after another the Connaughtmen and Ulstermen rose from their couches around the pig to boast of their exploits. When Cet mac Matach of Connaught drew his knife and stepped forward, he was challenged by Eogan Mor mac Durthacht. "Oh," said Cet, "I have seen you before. I took a drove of cattle right from in front of your house. The spear you threw stuck in my shield, and I took it and put out your eye." And One-Eyed Eogan sat down.

Then Munremur mac Gerrcind challenged Cet, and Cet answered, "Only three days ago I carried off three of your warriors' heads, together with the head of your first-born son," and Munremur fell silent. So it went, until suddenly the door flew open and in burst

A Celtic countenance, presumed to be that of a god, stares from a panel on a First Century B.C. bronze sacrificial vessel. Probably made in Central Europe and taken to Denmark, where it was found in 1845, the face is one of thousands that have been discovered throughout the Celts' realm, where the human head was revered as a symbol of life and power.

Ulster's most famous hero, Conall the Victorious, with a boast more sweeping than anything Cet could produce: Conall said that he had never passed a day of his life without killing at least one man from Connaught. So Conall carved the pig, taking the best part for himself and giving the Connaughtmen only the two forelegs. At this, the Connaughtmen rose in indignation and fell upon all the Ulstermen, causing blood to flow in seven streams through the seven doors of MacDatho's house.

Seeing there would be no bidding for his hound, MacDatho unleashed the animal and let it run to whichever side it chose. It ran to Ulster, but in the leave-taking of MacDatho's guests, the hound was struck by the royal charioteer of Connaught, and it died. And that, the story concludes, is how Ulster and Connaught fell out over MacDatho's dog and pig.

Stripped of its literary embroidery, this classic Celtic tale reflects the essence of a real world and a real people. Feasting, fighting and ritual boasting were typical of the Celts, an ancient, elusive people who occupied the center stage of Europe and the British Isles for about 800 years, between 700 B.C. and their almost complete assimilation into the Roman Empire around 100 A.D. Though their world is now dead, their culture influenced a good part of the Continent, and spread all the way from Ireland to the shores of the Black Sea.

The Celts seem a people of paradox. They held in their minds an image of an ideal heroic society, but they lived as prosperous cattlemen and farmers—often engaging in cattle theft. They worshiped gods who lived in sacred groves, but their sacrificial offerings to these deities included human heads. They admired skilled craftsmanship and intellectual prowess, but they were avid hunters and they fought each other at the drop of an insult—fiercely, and often for the sheer joy of physical combat.

During the period of their ascendancy, the Celts profoundly shaped the course of European history. They brought the knowledge of iron to the area north of the Alps and distributed its use through the length and breadth of their realm (pages 12-13). The Celts also introduced a number of important technological innovations to this part of Europe: with their iron plowshares, iron scythes and perhaps the earliest version of the reaping machine, the Celts established a pervasive pattern of intensive farming that is mirrored today in the lovingly tended countryside of Western Europe.

The Celts can also be credited with helping the peoples of Europe to become more mobile. With typical enterprise, they cut crude roads through the land and even paved some of them with timber, brushwood and stones. Over these roads rolled four-wheeled carts and two-wheeled chariots fitted with superior wheels of Celtic invention. The design called for a one-piece felly—or rim—of wood instead of the older type of rim fitted together from several separate parts; over the rim went a tight-fitting iron tire. The tire was, in effect, shrunk onto the rim while the metal was still hot (pages 24-25) by a process that later was forgotten and had to be reinvented.

Finally, the Celts fathered a number of modern peoples. Celtic blood, however much it may be diluted, runs in the veins of the English, the French and many Americans; and it runs abundantly in the Welsh, the Bretons, the Scots and especially the Irish. It is, for example, the part of the Frenchman that makes him Gallic. While the Celts in Gaul adopted

A Celtic Chronology

c. 1000-750 B.C.
Proto-Celtic people of the Urnfield culture dominate much of Continental Europe.

c. 700 B.C.
Early Celts in Austria bury iron swords with their dead.

c. 600 B.C.
Greeks found colony of Massilia, opening trade between Celts of inland Europe and the Mediterranean.

c. 500 B.C.
Trade between the Etruscans and Celts begins. La Tène phase of Celtic culture begins.

c. 400 B.C.
Celts invade Italy and settle Cisalpine Gaul.

390 B.C.
Raiding Celtic tribesmen ravage Rome.

c. 400-100 B.C.
La Tène culture spreads its distinctive art style over Europe to the British Isles.

279 B.C.
Celtic tribes invade Greece.

c. 275 B.C.
Celts establish state of Galatia in northern Turkey.

230 B.C.
Galatian Celts are defeated in battle by Greek forces from Pergamum, in western Turkey.

225 B.C.
A Roman army routs invading Celtic Gauls at Telamon in central Italy.

c. 200 B.C.
Permanent fortified settlements—oppida—spread from Gaul to Bohemia as population increases.

191 B.C.
Cisalpine Gaul is brought under Roman domination.

c. 100 B.C.
Belgae migrate from Continental Europe to Britain to escape harassment of Germanic tribes.

58-51 B.C.
Caesar's Gallic War subjugates most Celts on the Continent.

43 A.D.
Roman general Claudius begins the conquest of Britain.

432 A.D.
St. Patrick begins his mission to Christianize Ireland.

563 A.D.
St. Colum Cille founds the Celtic monastery on Iona.

590 A.D.
St. Columbanus establishes monastic and scholastic centers in Europe.

some of the customs of their Roman conquerors (having little choice in the matter), they nevertheless clung to the spirit of their own Celtic traditions. Take, for instance, Romanesque art, a style that reached its fullest development in medieval France: its motifs were liberally borrowed from the art of numerous predecessors—the Greeks, the Romans, the Byzantines and particularly the Celts (pages 53-61).

In history books the broad Celtic base that underlies so much of Western society is often given short shrift, partly because the earliest Celts did not believe in written records. Though their learned men, the Druids, could read and write Greek and Latin, they chose to pass on the chronicle of their people's existence orally in the form of verse. The poetry was not merely a literary device but a mnemonic one intended to fix the details of the stories in the Druids' memories. So strong was this tradition of an oral literature that none of the Celts' histories or laws were committed to paper until six or seven centuries after the birth of Christ; and then they were transcribed, fittingly enough, by the learned Celts of a later age, the Irish monks.

Apart from the lack of a written literature, the Celtic tradition in European history is difficult to trace because the Celts did not think of themselves as a single people. They spoke variants of the same language, and shared certain religious beliefs and a generic name, which the Greeks wrote as Keltoi and the Romans as Celtae. Nevertheless, they had no sense of nationhood to bind them together. The individual Celt was like a member of a present-day street gang in the sense that his allegiance was always to his tribe. And indeed, like street gangs, the Celtic tribes were often at war with one another. Because of this

lack of political unity in what was otherwise a culturally homogeneous world, it is not always easy to sort out the Celts from their non-Celtic neighbors —particularly from such near neighbors as the Teutons, a collection of Germanic-speaking tribes who lived in the areas to the north and east of the Celtic heartland on the European continent.

Yet, despite this amorphousness, there are many clear-cut clues to their identity, provided principally by ancient Irish literature. The story of MacDatho's dog and pig is only one of many Irish tales, all of them about the adventures of outsized heroes. The most famous collection of such legends is known as the Ulster Cycle, and it is thousands of years old. Generations of learned men memorized the tales and passed them down by word of mouth until they were finally transcribed, sometime after the Sixth Century A.D., by the literate Irish monks—perhaps out of pride in the traditional storytelling skill of their pagan Celtic ancestors.

Ireland in fact was, and still is, a honeycombed repository of information on the Celtic past. Its poetry and prose, as well as many of its customs and folkways, are full of material that is quintessentially Celtic. This is partly because Ireland was for many centuries almost untouched by outside influences. The Romans, their hands full in Britain, never attempted to send armies across the Irish Sea, and neither did the later Anglo-Saxons. And though the Vikings raided the island extensively and established trading towns on its coast, they never fully imposed their culture on the Irish people. Even the Roman Catholic Church in Ireland, for all its enormous influence on Irish life, adapted to the land and people, and became a peculiarly Celtic institution; in fact, it

A FAR-RANGING CELTIC WORLD

The tide of Celtic influence—measured across 800 years of raiding, conquest and colonization, and over some 800,000 square miles of Europe and Asia Minor—is charted on this map. The dark brown areas encompass the Celtic heartland, where ·the earliest identifiable Celtic culture developed during the Seventh and Sixth centuries B.C. The lighter brown areas mark the spread of the tribes and their cultural impact from that heartland across the European land mass, including areas as widely separated as Ireland and modern Turkey. From this maximum expanse in about 250 B.C., Celtic territory shrank, so that by Julius Caesar's time in the mid-First Century B.C. it encompassed only Gaul, a small part of the Iberian Peninsula and the British Isles. A century later, the Celtic culture survived only in Ireland, which was insulated from and never substantially affected by Roman influence.

BLACK SEA

Danube

REECE

AEGEAN
SEA

Delphi

was known in clerical circles as the Celtic Church.

The Irish, like the Welsh, preserved their Celtic heritage partly because they are a tenaciously conservative people. As late as the 16th Century A.D., for instance, when English statutes were officially the law of the land, there were still pockets of Ireland in which traditional Irish law was practiced. Codified and written down almost a thousand years before —just as the epic tales had been—these archaic laws went directly back to ancient Celtic times and were based on a tribal society in which men were responsible to one another rather than to the impersonal institution of a state. Thus wrongdoing was not a civil offense but a transgression of private rights, and a man who harmed another man paid his debt to the injured party's family, not to society as a whole.

Such respect for ancient tradition, however quaint it may seem to modern man, has made Ireland a lens through which scholars have been able to glimpse the dim and wavering outlines of a long-vanished world. But Ireland is not the only means of access to the Celtic past. Another view of it can be pieced together from the writings of the Celts' literate contemporaries, the Greeks and the Romans. Naturally, the Classical writers were chiefly concerned with those aspects of Celtic life that particularly intrigued, alarmed or interested the peoples of the Mediterranean. Just as naturally, they tended to observe the Celts, whom they regarded as barbarians, with something less than acute vision.

The Greeks and Romans knew the Celts first as consumers of their trade goods, especially their wine. "The Gauls," wrote Diodorus of Sicily in the First Century B.C., "are exceedingly addicted to the use of wine, and fill themselves with the wine which is brought into their country by merchants, drinking it unmixed." The Greeks and Romans also knew the Celts as warriors and found them ferocious fighters but somewhat simple-minded. "The whole race," wrote the Greek historian Strabo at about the same time, "is madly fond of war, high-spirited and quick to do battle. When they are stirred up, they assemble in their bands for battle quite openly and without forethought, so that they are easily handled by those who desire to outwit them."

For all their bias, it was the Classical writers who first examined the geography of the Celtic world and attempted to sort out the names and homelands of the various tribes. As early as 500 B.C., it had been generally acknowledged that Celtic peoples occupied the hinterlands north of the Mediterranean in a broad arc that swept from Spain to Eastern Europe; finally, Strabo put together for his readers a mosaic of tribal holdings in one segment of that arc, the land he called Celtica—the center of a region occupied by Celts that stretched all the way from Spain through the Balkans to the peninsula of Asia Minor.

The Roman name for that heartland was, of course, Gaul. Its boundaries, in Strabo's geographical survey, ran north from Iberia to the English Channel and east to the Rhine, and its southern border was defined partly by the Alps. The whole of the country was well watered by rivers, of which the most important was the Rhône, which passed through the most fertile land and flowed into the Mediterranean. The river was also navigable for large cargoes. Southern Celtica was capable of producing figs, olives, and grapes for wine; but as one moved north, the olive and the fig did not grow and the vine did not produce mature grapes. Nevertheless, no part of the land was un-worked except for swamps and thickets. This was because the women were fruitful and the population large, said Strabo, so that men were compelled to devote themselves assiduously to food production. Among their best crops were wheat and millet. The land also supported abundant quantities of live-stock—cattle, horses and pigs.

Within Celtica, Strabo counted no fewer than 60 tribes and subtribes. Along the Garonne River, which flows from the Pyrenees northwestward to the Atlantic, lived the Vivisci and the Santoni, who had established a lively trading center near the mouth of the river, at the modern site of Bordeaux. In western France, between the Garonne and the Loire, lay the territories of at least a dozen tribes, some of them quite affluent. The Petrocorii had ironworks, the Cadurci operated linenworks, and both the Ruteni and the Gabales were famous for their silver mines. And in central France, in the watershed of the Seine River, lived the Sequani, who produced some of the best salt pork imported by Rome.

In Strabo's ethnographic survey, the Rhineland rattled with the names of Celtic tribes: Helvetii, Treveri, Lingones, Leuci, Bellovaci and three tribes whose territories embraced a thickly forested area of small trees now called the Ardennes. When the Morini, Atrebatii and Eburones were attacked by enemies, wrote Strabo, they "used to intertwine the branches of brushwood, which were prickly, and thus block their passage; and in some places they fixed stakes in the ground, while they themselves penetrated into the depths of the forest with all their households."

The culture of the Classical writers who catalogued the Celtic tribal names—along with dozens of others —eventually incorporated all these peoples. In the

Text continued on page 19

The gigantic outline of a horse, nearly 350 feet long from head to tip of tail and cut into a chalk deposit underlying Uffington in southern England, is seen in its entirety from the air. The Celts who carved it, probably during the First Century B.C., may have regarded it as a symbol of a horse god.

Ancient Works Seen from the Air

Impressive even from the limited viewpoint of observers at ground level, many of the great earthworks, stone forts and other monuments left by the Celts are still more striking when seen by the airborne camera. The pictures on these pages, taken over England and Ireland, dramatically demonstrate how aerial photography can reveal the overall plan of a complex structure and clearly establish the relationship of the remnant's various parts to one another and to the surrounding terrain. Photographs like these, taken from aloft, also produce surprises: traces of such Celtic remains as house foundations or fences dividing fields, so faint that they might otherwise escape detection, are frequently picked up as shadowy outlines by a high-flying lens.

How the Celts followed the contours of a hill, girdling it with a series of concentric earthen ramparts and transforming it into a fortress, is clearly shown in the aerial photograph at left. Known today as Old Oswestry, the 2,000-year-old hill fort looms over the English terrain near the Welsh border.

Afternoon shadows boldly delineate the complex of structures on the 500-foot-high Hill of Tara, celebrated in Irish legend and history as the seat of heroic Celtic kings. Seen from aloft in broad perspective, the site northwest of Dublin has as its central feature a large oval rampart within which stand a pair of fortlike earthworks as well as a pre-Celtic burial mound.

Spectacularly located on the brink of a cliff high above the sea, the fortress of Dun Aengus on Inishmore, largest of Ireland's Aran Islands, was protected on its inland side by stout stone walls. As an added deterrent against attack, the Celts rimmed its approach with a field of jagged rocks.

Haystacks dot the fields in and around a circular enclosure known as a rath, a type of earthwork that ringed many farmsteads throughout Celtic Ireland. The rath probably was designed mainly to stave off cattle raids, which were commonplace events among the largely pastoral Irish during the Iron Age.

Most of the ridges that once neatly separated the fields of a Celtic farming community are still plainly evident in the valleys at Smacam Down in the south of England. But other ridges, like those that show up as faint shadowy lines in the left of the picture below, have been worn down into such gentle undulations that they might easily go unseen except for aerial photography.

process the Celts lost their identity, and it was not until the 16th Century A.D. that scholars began to re-establish it. A Scot named George Buchanan, studying the history of his country, established a link between the Celts of the Continent—whom he identified from Classical sources—and the peoples of Ireland and ancient Britain, including the Scots. A century later, Edward Lhuyd, a linguist, compiled a comparative etymology of the languages of Ireland, Wales, Brittany and Cornwall—an ancient province in southwestern England. He discovered that all four tongues had a common root, which he dubbed Celtic, borrowing Buchanan's term. Subsequently, "Celtic" came to be applied not only to the language but also to the culture of the people who spoke it.

The Celtic language is, in fact, an important clue to the Celts' common origin. Celtic is a branch of the language tree known as Indo-European, a tree that took root about 4,500 years ago somewhere between the Carpathian Mountains in Eastern Europe and the Ural Mountains in Russia. Indo-European is the most prolific language tree in the world. Various branches flowered into such tongues as Greek, Latin, Germanic, Slavic and Indic. Subsequently some of those limbs developed offshoots—Latin, for instance, gave rise to Italian, French, Spanish, Portuguese and Rumanian. Though an Englishman, a Russian and a Gaelic-speaking Irishman would have trouble understanding one another, their speech contains certain sounds indicating a common root for their languages. The Englishman says "one, two, three"; the Russian says "odin, dva, tri"; the Irishman says "aon, do, tri."

By the time the Greeks and Romans began to record the unfamiliar speech of their Celtic neighbors, it was already evident that their languages shared certain common elements. Celtic tribes living in different areas used similar words—for certain objects of trade, for example—and Celtic place names frequently bore identical endings. Modern scholars, tracing the frequency with which these endings occur in Classical writings, note that the word-ending *briga*, meaning "hill," occurs in some 70 places. It is attached to the names of Celtic settlements in Germany, France, Spain and Czechoslovakia. Similarly, the Celtic word for "fort," *dunum*, occurs in the names of more than 170 Celtic settlements mentioned by Greek and Roman writers. The *dunum* place names were scattered over Europe all the way from Greece to the British Isles—and some of them, such as Verdun and Dundee, survive to the present day. Because the distribution of these place names is so widespread, scholars are able to trace the patterns of Celtic origin and expansion. The Celts are thus assumed to be among the descendants of the early Indo-European settlers of the Continent, who first populated the Danube valley in the middle of the Third Millennium B.C. and then spread north and westward. (Oddly, at least one group of the Celts' predecessors may have traveled in the opposite direction, west to east, from a nebulous point of origin located somewhere on the Iberian Peninsula.)

Archeologists have since given these early Europeans names based on the places where the first traces of the people came to light, or on some cultural characteristic—a habit of burial, for instance, or a particular type of tool. One tribe from east of the Danube that acquired copper and moved into Central Europe in the Third Millennium is called the Battle-Ax people for the distinctive shaft-hole ax of metal or stone that is often found in their graves.

Foreshadowing what was to become the Celts' characteristic preoccupation with abstract patterns, middle Bronze Age potters decorated the clothing and faces of clay figurines with concentric circles, swirls and dots. These statues of women wearing bell-shaped skirts were unearthed during a 1955 cemetery excavation at Cîrna, in Rumania.

The Battle-Ax people were probably the first speakers of what scholars call proto-Indo-European, the ancestral language out of which evolved all the later tongues of this family. They are also the earliest European peoples who seem to have known about the wheel, and their habitual form of burial—under an earthen mound, or barrow—persisted in many parts of Europe down to the time of the Celts.

Meanwhile, other independent springs of cultural creativity were rising elsewhere in Europe. One such group surfaced somewhere on the Iberian Peninsula, possibly in Portugal, and flowed north and east, fanning out as it went to cover most of Western Europe and the British Isles. The carriers of this culture are called the Bell Beaker people for their characteristic bell-shaped clay cups. The Beaker folk learned their metallurgy on the Iberian Peninsula, where copper was plentiful, and they are credited with introducing the metalworking crafts throughout Western Europe.

Sometime after 2000 B.C., in Central and Eastern Europe, the Bell Beaker and Battle-Ax peoples apparently met and mingled, and a new culture was born. It is called Unetician for the Czech village of Unetice, where evidence of the culture was first unearthed. Unetician metalsmiths, combining locally mined copper and tin over fires forcibly heated by goatskin bellows, launched the European Bronze Age.

The Unetician metalworkers were fortunate to live in a centrally located area accessible to trade from all directions. To the south, passes led through the Alps to the Adriatic and northern Italy. To the north, the Elbe and Oder rivers gave access to the lands along the Baltic. Southeastward, the Danube connected the Uneticians with peoples along the Black Sea. Westward, the Central European plain stretched almost unbroken to the Channel ports and the British

Isles. Along these corridors of trade moved bronze goods, or rough-smelted copper and tin, in return for Irish gold, Cornish tin, and Baltic furs and amber.

Despite their affluence, the Uneticians lived simply. They had no grand cities, like the people of the Near East, but instead were clustered into small villages fortified by wooden stockades and surrounded by fields and pastures. There was some sort of tribal structure with chieftains and warriors to make decisions and man the fortifications. Probably their craftsmen enjoyed special status, being excused from work in the fields and from military duty. These class divisions were of long standing; they existed in all Indo-European societies. But the first reasonably clear evidence of such distinctions appears among the Uneticians, and as the Unetician culture expanded and spread westward across the Continent, it carried with it these class distinctions. Certainly this stratification of the social order was typical of later Celtic societies, whose classes performed functions associated with their particular social levels—functions that were obligatory. Chieftains, for instance, possessed rulers' rights, but in addition bore responsibilities for the safety and welfare of their people; they governed as aristocrats, but not as autocrats.

Along with class distinctions, another trademark of the Uneticians, also inherited by the Celts, was their burial practices. In a number of localities their dead were interred in chambers walled with wood, mounded over with round earthen barrows called tumuli. When the departed were important personages, they were often accorded special funerary treatment: their bodies were buried with gold and copper jewelry, and bronze daggers, halberds and battle-axes.

Around 1250 B.C. the latest of the cultural streams that nourished the birth of Celtic society began to spring up in Central Europe. Archeologists label these people the Urnfield culture for their practice of placing the ashes of their cremated dead in pottery urns, which were then set in collective burial plots. The Urnfield people were a lively, innovative folk who improved upon many of the practices of their Bronze Age predecessors. They harvested their crops with bronze sickles and used bronze carpentry tools to build log houses partitioned into rooms. They were fairly bursting with energy. When things got too quiet at home, their young men apparently hired themselves out as warriors to neighboring chieftains. As mercenaries they sallied forth bearing bronze body armor, shields and heavy slashing swords.

The Urnfield people moved into the valley of the Rhine, eventually across France and the Pyrenees, and even infiltrated the Alpine passes to settle in northern Italy. This was the region the Romans subsequently referred to as Cisalpine Gaul (Gaul-on-this-side-of-the-Alps) to distinguish it from Transalpine Gaul (Gaul-across-the-Alps).

The Urnfield folk boiled their meat in huge bronze cauldrons and washed it down with homemade beer or mead—a honey wine—served up in bronze drinking cups. They dressed in gay costumes woven with geometric designs. Tassels and pendants trimmed their belts and caps, and their shoulder capes and cloaks were decorated with bronze studs. They adorned themselves with bronze brooches, bracelets, and neck rings called torques. Urnfield potters made models—little decorated clay figurines—that turn up today in excavations in Yugoslavia and Rumania; their garments are not unlike more recent traditional peasant costumes of those regions.

With their vanity, their joy in eating and drinking and their precocity in the crafting of weapons and ornaments, the Urnfield people foreshadowed many of the qualities of their Celtic descendants. The Europe they inhabited was the one in which the Celts were soon to emerge. It was a Europe still fairly lightly settled, even well into the First Millennium B.C. Hawks wheeled over great expanses of forested wilderness, over the thatched roofs of the isolated farming villages that dotted patches of open land, over hamlets tucked into mountain passes. Here and there the landscape bore other marks of man, in the form of massive burial mounds. But there were no palaces, nor did Europe have any of the regal personnel that went with palaces: emperors, scholars, scribes, organized bodies of troops and troop commanders. It was a frontier world. Sovereignties existed only to organize tribal activities, and military activities were limited to raiding expeditions against neighboring tribes for their cattle or their land. But with its enterprising people, its widespread trading and the advantage of its mineral resources, Europe was pressing upon history.

The barrier broke around 700 B.C. By then some 1,500 years had elapsed since the Battle-Ax people had begun to migrate westward from the lower Danube basin. In that period, the great civilizations of the Near East were being destroyed. In Anatolia the Hittite Empire fell to unknown but wrathful invaders. In southern Greece the proud Mycenaeans had finally been all but wiped out by illiterate Dorian tribesmen from the north—and the region would live through six centuries of darkness before the Greece of Socrates arose. But in the West, young cultures were fermenting vigorously. In Italy the civilization of the Etruscans was establishing itself in modern Tuscany. And by 700 B.C., in the territory of the Urnfield people beyond the Alps, a new metal—iron —and its technology were finding congenial conditions for development. With the acquisition of skills in working iron, the so-called barbarian peoples of Europe took a giant stride forward: the turbulent drama of the Celts had begun.

Visit to a Vanished Way of Life

They built no cities, founded no empires and never developed a written language; as a result, the Celts have left only fragmentary traces of their vigorous passage through history. But by carefully piecing together the evidence drawn from archeological exploration, from the rich tales of Welsh and Irish folklore, and also from Greek and Roman histories, scholars can re-create Celtic life in some detail. Archeology provides telling clues, for instance, about how the Celts ran their farms; Classical authors detailed Celtic feasts; folk tales reflect much of Celtic religious customs; and objects from graves reveal some of the Celts' thoughts on death.

As to the Celts' appearance, a saga recorded in the Eighth Century A.D. establishes an intriguing portrait of Edaín, the loveliest girl in Ireland. From the legend comes this litany of her charms: "Her upper arms were as white as the snow of a single night, and they were soft and straight; and her clear and lovely cheeks were as red as the foxglove of the moor . . . . The bright blush of the moon was in her noble face; the lifting of pride in her smooth brows; the ray of love-making in both her royal eyes; a dimple of sport in both her cheeks . . . . She was the fairest and loveliest and most perfect of the women of the world that the eyes of men had ever seen; they thought she must be of the fairies."

In a sunlit glade, the beautiful Edaín admires herself in a polished bronze mirror, as her handmaiden combs out her red-gold locks so that the lady may wash her hair. Golden embroidery embellishes the hem and the breast of her green silk dress, and gold jewelry adorns her neck, her arms and a coil of hair on top of her head. A robe of purple wool lies across her lap. The broad silver washbasin at her feet is decorated with flashing purple carbuncles and golden insets.

Autumn Tasks on a Farm

A Celtic farm family works to finish postharvest chores before the onset of winter. The farm's master and his son (left) prepare to fit a red-hot iron tire over the rim of a cart wheel made of a single bent piece of ashwood. As the tire cools, it will contract to fit tightly onto the wheel. Two of the women (background, left) place next spring's seed on a roofed platform. A servant (above) scoops harvested grain into a storage pit, while another feeds the pigs. Two youths repair the house's roof while a third patches a wall.

To the archeologist, faint scratchings in the soil and shallow postholes become solid pieces in the puzzle of reconstruction. Systematic excavation of circular farmsteads in southern England—and painstaking correlation of the finds at each of them—has revealed much of the life of prosperous Celtic farmers in the First Millennium B.C.

In most cases, foundation postholes for circular dwellings remain on the farm sites, and lined pits for storing grain tell of provision made for cold winters, while iron plowshares give evidence of advanced agricultural methods. Traces of ditches surrounding tracts as large as six acres suggest defensive fortifications as well as barriers to corral livestock, whose bones have been found in refuse heaps.

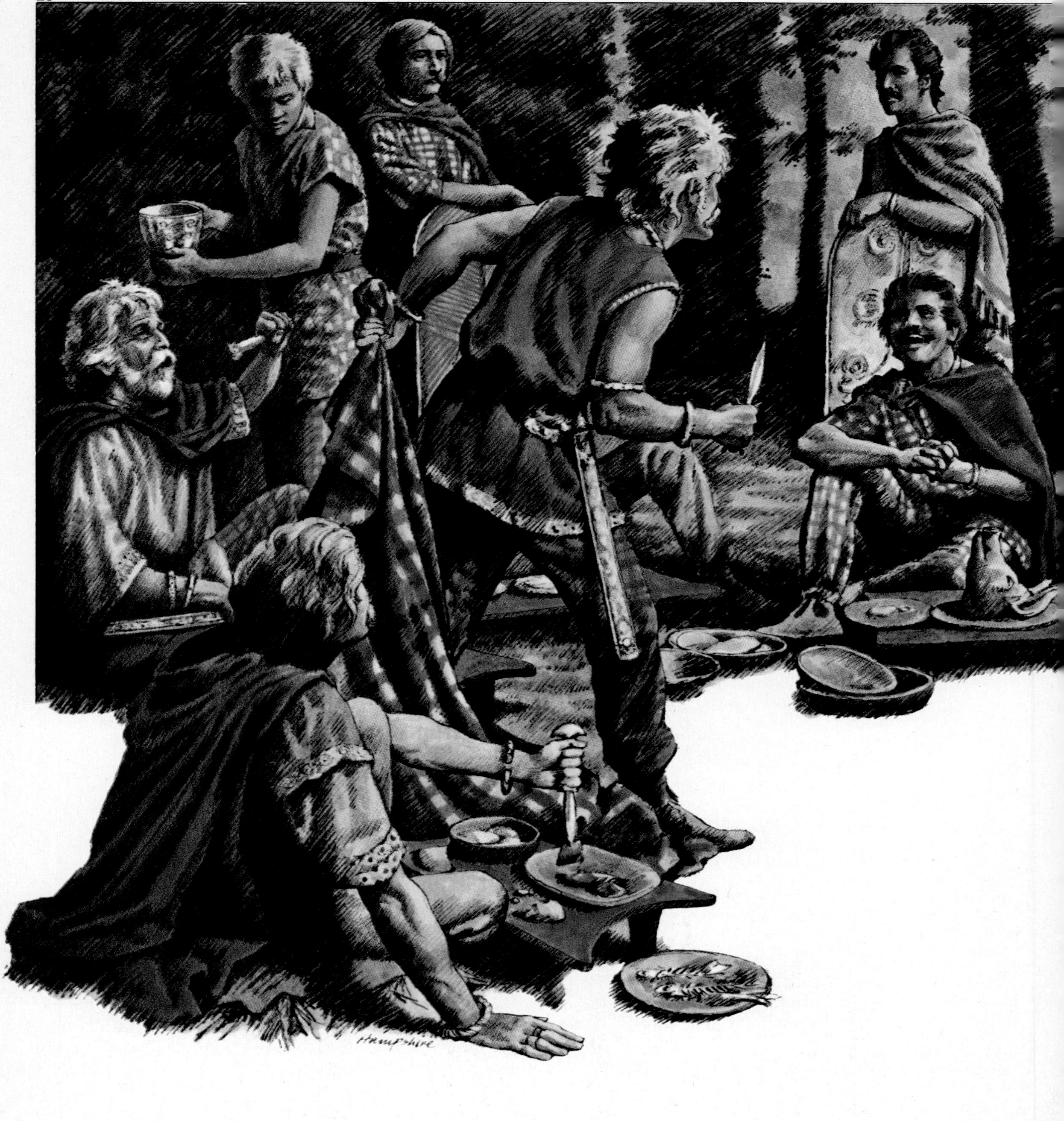
Hampshire

Heated Tempers at a Victory Feast

In the midst of a victory feast, a young warrior—goaded beyond endurance by the jeers of his opponent (right) in a boasting match—menaces his tormentor with a knife. The man seated at left complacently spears his food, while his neighbor—a gray-bearded elder being served wine in the single cup passed among the banqueters—watches the action in amusement. The host, seated at center before the main dish of roast boar, raises his arm to caution prudence. At his right, the guest of honor eggs on the young hothead.

The feasting habits of the Celts fascinated Greek and Roman observers, especially on those occasions when the dinner party turned violent. Participants in a feast drank undiluted wine, and according to Diodorus, the First Century B.C. Sicilian who documented them, "When they become drunk, they fall into a stupor or into a maniacal rage."

At the feast, often a celebration after a victory in battle, warriors could boast of their deeds. The leading chieftain rewarded the most convincing competitor with the "hero's portion," usually the haunch of a fine boar. But among the losers, wrote the Greek commentator Posidonius, anger at their loss of face might lead to a deadly assault on the winner—unless the host or other guests stepped in to break up the quarrel.

Propitiating the Pastoral God

One important Celtic religious event was the May Day festival of Beltaine, marking summer's beginning. According to Irish lore, the Druids, or priests, invoked the god of herd and harvest to ensure prolific herds and abundant crops. Beltaine was in many ways like a modern religious festival, combining solemn rites with a joyful feast, a fair and a day of sports.

The eve of Beltaine, however, was a dangerous and unsettling time: in the night dividing spring from summer, luck could turn and cattle become bewitched—unless the Druids placated the god with gifts and incantations. The Celtic belief that severed heads could plead for the living made them a worthy sacrifice to Belenos. And because fire was sacred, cattle driven through the purifying smoke of bonfires were assured health and fecundity.

At dawn, Druids complete the rites that will bring a fruitful year. As cattle pass between bonfires of oak and green yew, topped by maypoles (above), symbolizing the sacred oak tree, a Druid by the fire offers sacred cakes to the harvest god, entreating him to purify the beasts with the pungent smoke. At the right, beneath oak branches hung with torques and bracelets offered by the faithful, the chief Druid lifts his arms in prayer to an image of the god, while a younger seer, kneeling, divines omens from a human skull.

30

A Splendid Burial for a Princess

Because the Celts believed in burying the dead with all their wealth for the journey to the afterlife, their graves have provided exceptionally rich archeological finds. It was obligatory, especially for the noble classes of Celtic society, to be interred with the finest gold, silver and bronze they possessed, along with such special funerary equipment as finely wrought wagon biers for the dead to lie upon.

One grave, unearthed in 1953 near Vix in central France, was particularly exciting to archeologists: the 2,500-year-old tomb of a princess, it included not only objects of Celtic origin but also imported artifacts such as a 350-pound wine jar from Greece—proof of trade between the Mediterranean world and remote northern Gaul as early as 500 B.C.

Mourners gaze for the last time at a dead princess and the sumptuous treasure that will accompany her into the grave. At left, a man admires an immense bronze wine vessel of Greek manufacture. The corpse, lying in a ceremonial cart that has been dismantled, wears a golden diadem also fashioned by Greeks, although the rest of her jewelry was wrought by Celts. Attendants tenderly adjust the leather sheet that will be her shroud. Others lower two of the detached wagon wheels into the open grave.

High above the tiny Austrian market town of Hallstatt, which hugs the shores of an Alpine lake, towers the Salzberg—literally "salt mountain." From it men have been taking salt since long before recorded time. Probably the mountain's treasure was first discovered by primitive hunters tracking their game to saline springs, where crystals collecting on the rocks provided a natural lick.

By the end of the Bronze Age, in the Eighth Century B.C., the Hallstatt mines were being worked fairly intensively, since salt was a valuable commodity. Using bronze picks, wedges and chisels, men bored as much as 1,200 feet into the mountainside, carving precarious tunnels that had to be shored up with timbers. Some were furnished with tree-trunk steps for the miners to negotiate steep inclines.

In the centuries that followed, men working the Hallstatt mine occasionally came upon objects used or worn by these early miners, kept more or less intact by the preservative action of the mineral: stiff pieces of clothing—leather mittens, leather leggings and caps; the shriveled leaves of *Pestwurt,* a medicinal herb still commonly used in the area as a folk remedy for miners' ills—and the charred remnants of bundled sticks employed by the miners as torches. Now and then there were traces of prehistoric meals —remains of animal bones.

In 1846 the man then in charge of the Hallstatt

Once the highly prized possession of a wealthy Celtic woman, this bronze mirror is engraved on its back with an abstract pattern of swirling tendrils, inspired by natural branches and leaves. The work of a master artist-craftsman from the First Century B.C., the mirror, unearthed in an 1908 during an industrial excavation at Desborough in central England, represents the highest development of the most sophisticated Celtic art style.

mines, George Ramsauer, became intensely curious about these ancient miners and began to search for other signs of them. His investigations led to a stunning discovery: a burial site containing almost a thousand graves. The find launched Ramsauer on what was to become a 17-year preoccupation. Using a good bit of his own money and whatever time he could borrow from his job (as well as from his paternal duties to the 24 children in his family), Ramsauer systematically opened and noted the contents of 993 graves in a carefully kept diary.

The contents of these burial places revealed a prosperous community whose members were skilled in ironwork, who traded widely with Scandinavians, Etruscans and Greeks, among others; it was clear that the people of the settlement were also warriors and horsemen, as well as gifted carpenters and artists. The burial sites, and others like them found by later archeologists working in the surrounding area, are generally believed to be those of early Celts. And still other graves, found in places ranging from France to Czechoslovakia, have been identified as belonging to Celts of the same period.

The oldest such graves have been dated from 700 B.C.—by which date the Iron Age in Central Europe was already underway— and the people buried in them obviously lived during a period of cultural transition. Some of the bodies were cremated in the Urnfield fashion, but at least half of them were skeletons. Some of the sites contained four-wheeled funerary wagons, reminiscent of the wagon-wheel burials of the Battle-Ax folk, although Battle-Ax graves never included the wagons themselves.

Even more intriguing, many of the graves of the Hallstatt period contained horse fittings and harness ornaments—an early indication of the importance the people gave to their horses. Since the graves with horse gear were rich in other goods too, experts assume they belonged to the community's elite.

Apart from the wagons and horse fittings, the Hallstatt-period graves held other fascinations for archeologists. Bronze wine flagons and cauldrons of sophisticated Greek and Etruscan design, necklaces of Scandinavian amber and sword hilts inlaid with imported gold and ivory pointed to an affluence based on trade of considerable dimensions. Even more fascinating, many of the weapons—swords, daggers, spearheads, battle-axes—were made of a material new to graves of the region: iron.

Taking their first look at the graves in the Hallstatt cemetery, scholars thought that the iron objects, like the other artifacts, were imports. Later they decided that the design and craftsmanship were unique and probably indigenous. Certainly iron ore was available from the mines nearby in the eastern Alps, which were widely known in the ancient world. But the route by which iron technology reached the region must have been long and circuitous.

In the Near East, metalsmiths had known about iron for centuries: the Hittites were producing and marketing iron objects as far back as 1500 B.C. But from the end of the Hittite Empire in 1200 B.C. to the first-known appearance of iron in Central Europe, about 700 B.C., lies a period in the history of iron technology about which archeologists can only guess. Though numerous iron objects have been found in Near Eastern sites that can be dated from this puzzling 500-year void, clues to the development and spread of the ironworking art from the Near East are virtually nonexistent.

Yet, however the skill arrived in Central Europe, it must have been well received. From previous experience with copper and bronze and with a natural aptitude for technological pursuits, the metalworking peoples north of the Alps quickly became competent ironworkers. They learned how to mine the ore, how to crush and combine it with layers of charcoal and how to heat the ore until it became a blackened sponge, or bloom. They learned how to hammer the bloom to remove the cinders, or slag—a process that rarely, and only inadvertently, resulted in a carburizing of the metal to produce a kind of rudimentary steel. They learned how to forge the hot iron into a variety of shapes by repeatedly heating it and hammering it while it was malleable.

These first European blacksmiths were not only apt students, they were also particularly fortunate in having an abundance of raw material right in the immediate vicinity. In some areas iron was abundant not only in rich veins but in bogs—marshy depressions in the earth's surface—where smiths could simply dredge it up. In fact, the metal was so easy to come by that it soon generated a flourishing industry, and iron weapons became as popular as those made of bronze.

Wherever it has appeared throughout history, iron has changed the way of men. It has given them new tools to build with, new weapons to cut each other down with. Iron is expansionist; it rolls over hills and fields, hacks through forests, destroys boundaries. In the several centuries after the first appearance of the metal among the Celtic peoples living in the Austrian Alps, iron was responsible for spreading their culture throughout Europe and across the Eng-

In a painting by Austrian artist Isidor Engl, Lake Hallstatt lies surrounded by mountains near Salzburg. During the mid-19th Century a vast cemetery, honeycombed with the graves of some of the earliest Celts, was discovered on the mountain rising at the center.

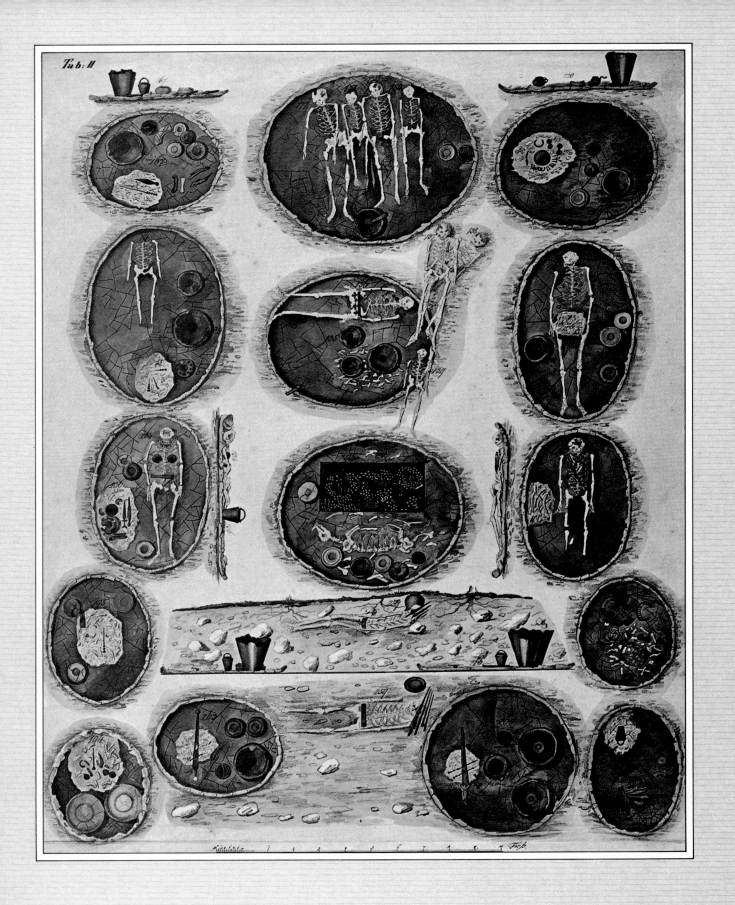

Tab: II

These Hallstatt graves were drawn by artist Isidor Engl, who meticulously recorded their contents. The numbers penned on the drawings indicate the order in which the tombs were excavated by their Austrian discoverer, George Ramsauer. Most of them contained simple utilitarian objects such as pots and weapons; but grave No. 132, near the center, also yielded quantities of finery, including rings and other ornaments made of gold or bronze.

lish Channel into all parts of the British Isles.

Sometimes the culture was imposed by force. Bands of chariot-mounted Celtic warriors, led by chieftains who were in effect warlords, regularly engaged in forays against their neighbors. Sweeping down on isolated settlements, brandishing their long iron slashing-swords, they must have been a terrifying sight, especially to people unfamiliar with either their weapons or their tactics. The warriors were out for land, cattle, slaves—and whatever other booty they could lay their hands on. Yet their raiding was as much an exercise in manhood as an attempt at material gain.

Indeed, the Celtic culture was probably spread just as widely by farmers and herdsmen. Pushed from their hereditary lands, probably by an expanding population combined with a need for fresh soil to cultivate, they moved in among other peoples, taking with them such technological improvements as a heavy plow with an iron share, which the Celts eventually introduced to the rest of Europe. This implement was far more efficient than the existing wooden plowshare, which could only score the ground; with the iron plowshare it was possible to break up the soil and to put even heavy clay soils under cultivation. Furthermore, it helped farmers to turn under topsoil depleted by past crops and bring to the surface rich soil to nourish future crops.

The Celts also brought with them advanced ideas in carpentry, which they could apply to boatbuilding, deftly wielding adzes to fashion masts, oars and the planks that made up the hulls of seaworthy vessels. But most of their woodworking skill went into the construction of elaborate fortifications to protect their settlements from the constant raiding that was

a feature of Celtic life. The earliest versions of these fortifications, called hill forts, were placed on high ground, for obvious reasons, and usually they operated more like army garrisons than ordinary towns. Though the nobility sometimes lived in them, along with such respected craftsmen as smiths, the hill forts were primarily places of temporary refuge. Farmers and herdsmen crowded into them along with their families and their animals when their lands were under attack from marauding Celtic tribesmen.

The walls of the hill forts were massive earthwork affairs braced internally with timber supports. A ditch surrounded the outside wall, and inside, the few dwellings were sometimes built directly against the wall, lending it extra support. Archeologists studying the construction of one such hill fort near Abernethy, Scotland, estimated that its carpenters had used 3,200 linear feet of nine-inch-wide lumber for the internal support of a wall that enclosed about an eighth of an acre. To do so, they had to fell some 640 trees of suitable size, a logging operation that must have covered some 60 acres of forest.

By the Sixth Century B.C. these assertive, technologically precocious Celts had come to dominate most of France and the Low Countries, and they had pushed over the Pyrenees to establish Celtic enclaves in Spain. By the Fourth Century B.C. they had crossed the English Channel to intrude themselves on the indigenous peoples living along the lower reaches of the Thames. But the center of their power eventually established itself in an area roughly composed of what is now Switzerland, western Austria, southern Germany and France.

In this heartland—especially in the lush valleys of the Seine, Rhône, Rhine and upper Danube—the Celt-

Salt: A Primary Source of Wealth

For the early Celts of Austria, during the Hallstatt period from 700 B.C. to 500 B.C., one of the main sources of wealth was the salt buried in the Alpine mountains. Valued as a food preservative as well as a flavoring, the salt in the Austrian Alps had been a rich resource as early as Paleolithic times, and the deposits the early Celts worked still yield an abundance of the prized mineral.

To extract this treasure from the mountainsides, the Celts burrowed molelike through rock and clay, and crept down slanting shafts more than 1,000 feet long to the cavernous salt deposits. Timber supports shored up the shafts, and notched logs supplied footholds for the descending miners. But the work was cold and treacherous; within the mines the temperature often sank to just above freezing, and the air was heavy with smoke from the pine torches the miners wedged into the walls for illumination.

Dressed for warmth, the miners pried the salt from the mine faces, collected it with wooden scoops and transported it in cowhide backpacks. At first the miners worked alone, later they worked in teams. The signs of their industry are still visible today: scraps of leather and wood, broken tools, the remains of meals eaten on the job. In the mines' saline atmosphere materials that normally crumble to dust have lasted for millennia.

Backpack slung over his shoulder, pickax in hand, a Celtic salt miner trudges off to work. His leather pouch holds bundles of pine twigs to use as flares for light; homeward bound, his cargo will be salt. Withes interwoven around the top of the pouch hold it open, and the handle is a wooden baton. The mine's intense cold necessitates warm clothing: woolen shirt and breeches, leather footgear, a sheepskin cap.

Two Celtic miners work in tandem—one holding a pickax and
the other wielding a wooden mallet—to chip a heart-shaped
outline into a wall of salt. Next they will score the heart
down the middle and pry both sections from the wall. Using
this highly efficient two-man approach, the work was so
steady that the men, warmed by their exertion, could doff some
of their heavy clothes. The curve of the pickax handle has
a special purpose: it dissipates the force of the mallet blows,
helping the pickman to hold the ax steady. Even so, the impact
of the hammer blows and the brittleness of the rock-hard salt
shattered many an ax; broken ax points still litter many mines.

ic tribes flourished, and their nobility grew immensely rich. Celtic princes and princesses were buried amid even greater splendor than that revealed in the Hallstatt graves.

Spurred by the demands of these wealthy patrons, and inspired by the artisanship of imported luxury goods, Celtic craftsmen turned out wares of increasingly sophisticated design. In fact, a distinctive Celtic art came into existence, one that fascinates archeologists as well as art historians. By tracing the course of the art's development through various stylistic conventions, and by noting its geographical spread, they can chart the Celts' movements across the map of Europe with a fair degree of accuracy.

The first phase of Celtic art, which lasted from about 700 B.C. to 500 B.C., is called Hallstatt for the Alpine village where the first identifiable Celtic graves were found. During the Hallstatt period, when the art style spread no farther than the vague boundaries of the Western European Celtic heartland, the designs used by Celtic craftsmen basically reflected their inheritance from earlier European traditions. The motifs were taken from nature, but they were stylized. When human figures appear, they are often so sketchy as to be almost abstract. One nameless potter whose work was found in a grave near Sopron, Hungary, decorated his pots with drawings of men and women done primarily in squares, circles and triangles. Yet the drawings themselves are far from static, and indeed form a lively social commentary.

The Sopron potter's women wear short bell-shaped skirts, and they are engaged in spinning, weaving, dancing, playing the lyre and riding horseback. In one scene, two of them are pulling each other's hair. The potter's men—most of them in fighting scenes—wear long trousers, or breeches, a style of dress so strange to the eyes of southern European peoples that it later became, for Greeks and Romans, one of the identifying marks of the Celts.

The artists of the Hallstatt period drew birds and animals with considerably greater realism and far more grace than they did their human figures. Swans and ducks seem especially to have delighted the artisans. Indeed, water birds decorated so many different kinds of objects, from bronze vessels to wagon shafts, that scholars think the birds may have been associated with some sort of religious cult. (Swan maidens and swan hunts are mentioned frequently in ancient Irish legends.) Also in the Hallstatt artists' repertoire were goats and stags, and one vessel's lid even includes the image of a sphinx, a mythical beast with a man's head and a lion's body. The concept of these creatures was imported from the Greeks, who put them on jars sold to the Celts. The creator of the design on the vessel lid may have copied the figures from those he saw on a Greek import—or perhaps he himself was a Greek artisan in the service of a Celtic chieftain.

In addition to the bird and animal motifs, which may or may not be cult symbols, Hallstatt artisans occasionally produced objects that clearly had a ritual purpose, though the precise religious significance is generally very difficult to pin down. One of the most famous of such objects is a miniature bronze wagon found in a Seventh Century B.C. grave at a Celtic site in Strettweg, Austria. On the wagon, which is roughly 14 inches long by 7 inches wide, the sculptor arranged two almost identical groups of figures back to back, facing away from the center. In each group,

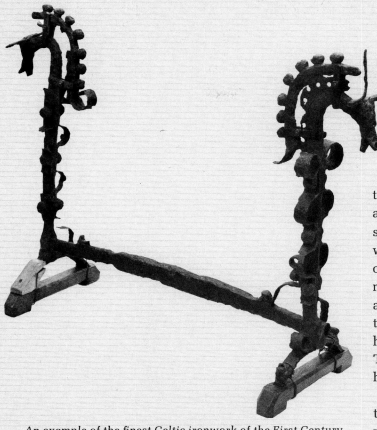

An example of the finest Celtic ironwork of the First Century A.D., this andiron—found in Wales and standing about 30 inches high—may have supported the great logs that burned during feasts in the home of a chieftain. Each of its uprights is capped by a stylized oxhead with an ornate crest; the ribbon-like loops riveted to the uprights probably held bars upon which rested spits used for roasting joints of meat.

two figures stand on the axles, holding between them a stag with a splendid spread of antlers. Behind them, standing on the wagon bed, are two pairs of mounted warriors wearing pointed helmets; between the pairs of warriors are two other figures—a woman and a man, both naked. In the center of the wagon stands a single figure, a woman, presumably a goddess. She towers above the other figures and supports above her head on her upraised arms a large, shallow bowl. The goddess, too, is naked except for a belt around her waist and a pair of earrings.

Whatever its symbolism—some scholars guess that the group relates to a ritual sacrifice—the Strettweg wagon is typical of Hallstatt design. The figures are slender and attenuated, spare and somewhat stiff; yet the stiffness is more a matter of artistic convention than lack of skill. In spirit, they are rather like archaic Greek art, and perhaps that is the source of the artist's inspiration. Certainly wealthy Celtic patrons knew about the Aegean world and its products—especially Greek wine.

The demand among the Celts for Greek wine was, in fact, responsible for the abundance of one particular kind of artifact: richly painted jars for storing and serving the beverage. Sometimes these containers still hold the dregs of their former contents. In one case a massive vessel with a 280-gallon capacity was found in the grave of a rich Celtic princess at Vix, near Châtillon-sur-Seine, some 300 miles north of the Greek colonial port city of Massilia, now Marseille, where the wine from Greece was transshipped.

The princess of Vix was buried around 500 B.C. Though the objects of Celtic manufacture buried with her belonged to the Hallstatt period, another sort of Celtic art was already emerging to the north and east

Early Artifacts of Intricate Design

Although the Celts were usually portrayed by Greek and Roman writers as barbarians—ever spoiling for a fight—they were in fact a remarkably creative people. Refining motifs inherited from their Bronze Age predecessors or borrowing ideas and techniques from neighboring cultures, they developed a strikingly distinctive art based largely on forms found in nature.

The pottery and bronze objects illustrated on these pages are examples of the initial phase of that art, spanning the period from about 700 to 500 B.C. and known as the Hallstatt style after an early Celtic site in Austria. Hallstatt art, like much of the more sophisticated art produced by later Celts, tended to be abstract—favoring zigzags, concentric circles and other geometric designs, or stiffly stylized figures of animals and birds.

A four-inch-wide bronze brooch from a Hallstatt grave in Austria, with its row of triangle-and-chain pendants, was obviously designed to delight the Celtic wearer's ear as well as his eye. The concentric rings that dot the brooch's crescent-shaped middle segment may be representations of sun disks.

Boldly decorated with incised and impressed geometric designs, this pottery vessel in the Hallstatt style, found in western Germany, is nearly 15 inches in diameter. The blackened effect was achieved by a coating of graphite.

The bronze cart above, only 10 inches high and fashioned by a
Hallstatt artisan, may be a miniature of the type used in
rituals. The ducks adorning it probably had a mystical meaning,
since for the Celts many birds were symbols of divinity.

A combination vessel and stand (right), about 14 inches high overall, comes from a rich grave at Hallstatt. Made of sheet bronze, it was probably meant for use in rituals. The twisted, crossing struts between the legs of the stand are a feature that may have been borrowed from the art of Iron Age Italy, but the rest of the decoration is typical of the Hallstatt style. The slender stylized figures of waterfowl swim up each leg toward the vessel, which is embossed with other water birds and disks that may be sun signs.

Another burial site at Hallstatt yielded this bronze bowl, whose handle is a cow followed by her calf; both figures are of solid bronze. The forelegs of the six-inch-long cow are supported by a metal brace riveted to the bowl.

of where she lived. It was to last well into Christian times and to spread all over the Celtic world, from the Black Sea to Ireland.

Unlike the severe and restrained Hallstatt art, the new Celtic art was flamboyant and curvilinear and, at its height, dazzling in the complexity of its design. Apparently it found immediate favor with the bold and self-assured Celtic aristocrats, for it rapidly became the dominant Celtic art style.

The distinctness of this style demanded a name, and archeologists dubbed it La Tène, for a site at the end of Lake Neuchâtel, Switzerland, where the first extensive collection of objects decorated in the style was found. In 1857, the lake in one of its periodic changes fell to an unusually low level, and spectral timbers appeared above the waterline. They attracted the attention of a well-to-do amateur archeologist of the region, Colonel Friedrich Schwab, who assumed they were the pilings of Swiss lake dwellings dating from the Stone Age. Swiss lake dwellings were the colonel's specialty. For more than three years he dredged the site with a boat and a scoop he had specially designed for the purpose. From the boat he could observe the shallow lake bottom, and with the scoop he could lift fragile objects still encased in a protective block of mud, so as not to damage them in the dredging process.

Altogether the colonel lifted hundreds of iron weapons from the lake bottom, prompting later archeologists to decide that La Tène had been a votive site. The spectral timbers—it turned out—were not pilings but the supports of a bridge spanning a river flowing into the lake, and people crossing the bridge had thrown offerings over its edge, perhaps to placate the water spirits they believed dwelt beneath the water's surface.

Among the La Tène weapons were 50 long, slim swords with intriguing designs on their blades just below the hilt. Instead of being stiff and geometrical, they were done in swirling lines that curled into tendrils and looped into whorls and spirals. Subsequently, at other Celtic excavations in the valleys of the Rhine and the Marne, similar configurations were found, convincing scholars that the La Tène designs, far from being simply a local phenomenon, represented a major cultural turnaround. What did these patterns mean, and where did they come from?

La Tène art resembles to a certain degree the art of the Scythians of south Russia, a people with whom the Celts can scarcely have had much contact. Did stray examples of Scythian art find their way into Europe through some intermediary and catch the eye of some especially gifted Celtic artisan, a kind of Celtic Picasso, who then inspired a whole school of followers? Perhaps. Since La Tène art, always quite widely distributed, nevertheless came to be polished and perfected in one very localized region, some scholars think the original impetus may have come from the workshop of one particular man, a master craftsman so skillful that he influenced generations of other craftsmen. He is called, somewhat romantically, the Master of Waldalgesheim after the site on the middle Rhine where the most typical examples of his work have been found. So strong was his influence that, instead of La Tène, the style might have carried the name of his birthplace—Waldalgesheim.

Waldalgesheim art set the tone for the two other versions of La Tène art that followed it: the plastic style and the sword style. Ideally every part of the object was covered with design—the more fantastic and convoluted the design, the better. Giving free rein to his imagination, the Master of Waldalgesheim and other practitioners of his style filled every available inch of surface with trailing and twining flowers, looping stems and curling leaves, strange masklike faces, and whorls ending in solitary eyes.

In the La Tène art called plastic, this concept is translated into three dimensions, shaping the very contours of the object into elaborate openwork patterns. And in sword art, Waldalgesheim design is superimposed on straightforward figurative drawings to create an art that is at once abstract and representational. For example, in sword art (so called because it appears most often as decoration on sword scabbards) the figure of a horse is recognizable in outline only. Within the outline, the body of the animal is patterned with designs that have only a fleeting relation to such items as saddle and bridle and, likewise, little or no connection to the muscles and bones of the equine anatomy.

La Tène art is not a comfortable art. Much of it seems like material drawn from the dream world; and like dreams it is vaguely disquieting. There is, for example, a beautiful bronze flagon from Dürrnberg, Austria, with a slender spout patterned in filigree and a gracefully curved handle that is actually the arching body of a catlike animal. The workmanship is elegant and the design a delight, until suddenly one notices that the animal's jaws hold a severed human head. On two bronze flagons from Basse-Yutz in Lorraine, fantastic beasts form the handles; but their leap carries them toward unsuspecting ducks that are sitting placidly on the flagon spout, completely unaware of their imminent danger.

GEOMETRIC GLIMPSES OF CELTIC LIFE

Although abundant artifacts and bones of the Iron Age Celts came to light after excavation began at Hallstatt in 1846, scholars hoped for a glimpse of the people themselves. The long-awaited Celtic self-portrait finally was discovered in a hoard of decorated pottery at Sopron, Hungary, around 1900. Buried in hillside barrows, these funerary urns were decorated with lively scenes of daily pursuits, which are redrawn here in slightly reduced form. The vignettes offered a fleeting view of Celtic activities both religious and secular, yet their stylized design reveals little of the personalities of the people.

Going about their business like animated puppets, denizens of early Sopron, wearing striated, bell-shaped costumes, take part in a religious ceremony. The two bird-faced figures (top) seem to be sacrificing a horned animal over an altar, while a worshiper (above, left), adorned with curls or jewelry, dances as if in a trance. Directly above, a horseman—apparently an onlooker—holds onto the bridle of his round-hoofed mount.

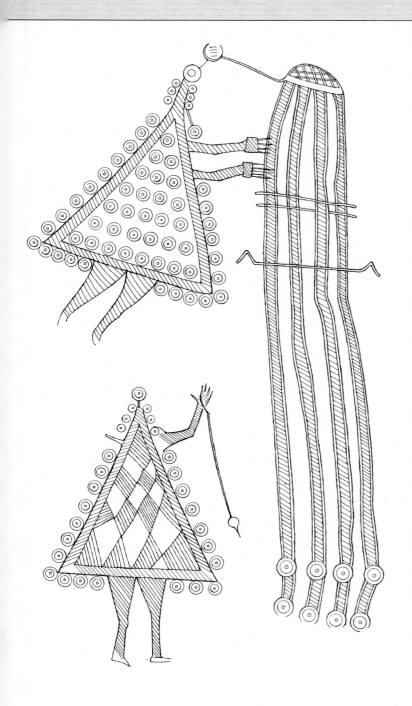

Two women, gaily attired in conical dresses covered with concentric circles and checkerboard designs, are busily creating some of the renowned textiles of the Hallstatt period. The maypole-like shape is a loom; the figure at the top, with only a circle to suggest its head, is probably weaving some woolen fabric. At the bottom, a spinner swings a spindle that twists the fibers into yarn to be used in sewing garments.

As La Tene art matured, the cryptic quality of its designs became even more pronounced. Nothing was ever quite what it seemed to be. A marvelously intricate openwork bronze ornament from a grave in Czechoslovakia is dominated by what appears to be the splendid head of a bull. But when the head is viewed from another angle, it is seen to have a human face. Similarly, on an iron-plated chariot fitting found in Champagne, a spiral scroll running in a pattern around the piece repeatedly delineates and then dissolves the outlines of a human face, so that in the end the face seems like an apparition.

By the Second Century B.C., La Tène design had developed into an art form so distinctively Celtic that, whatever its derivations and borrowings, it had almost nothing in common with the art of other contemporary peoples. La Tène was, for instance, far more concerned with the natural world than was the humanistic art of the Greeks—particularly as it confronted the more savage aspects of nature. Paul Jacobsthal, one of the foremost scholars of Celtic art, called it both "attractive and repellent, elaborate and clever; full of paradoxes, restless, puzzlingly ambiguous; rational and irrational; dark and uncanny. Yet it was a real art." This description applies as well to the people for whom the art was made.

During their long centuries of affluence—through both the Hallstatt and La Tène periods—the Celts in the north butted against the territories of the Teutons in Scandinavia. In the west they occupied all of Britain right up to the north of Scotland. Small numbers of Celts inhabited Ireland as early as 500 B.C. and continued to migrate there from the Continent and from Britain, with a last wave entering from Britain—perhaps as a result of the Roman invasions of Britain in the First Century B.C.

In the south, attracted by the riches of the Etruscan world—and no doubt by the climate that has immemorially drawn northern Europeans to the "land of the lemon trees"—they crossed the Alps to raid Italy, sacking Rome in 390 B.C. Though they retreated from this excursion almost immediately, they did establish a foothold in northern Italy.

In the east, Celtic tribes pushed down the Danube as far as Bulgaria, where raiding Celts came in contact with Alexander the Great, who was operating in the same area. Alexander received envoys from these Celts in 335 B.C. and exchanged pledges of alliance with them. Reportedly, the Celtic oath mentioned that their allegiance to Alexander would last "until the sky fell down." Perhaps this was a version of the vow used by Celts in Ireland 1,000 years later: "We will keep faith unless the sky fall and crush us or the earth open and swallow us or the sea rise and overwhelm us."

With the dissolution of Alexander's empire after his death in 323 B.C. and with the riches of Greece to draw them on, Celtic warriors pushed south into Macedonia and in 279 B.C. marched into Greece itself. From there a few of the more venturesome tribes crossed the Hellespont into Asia Minor and moved inland to establish the Celtic kingdom of Galatia, near modern Ankara. The descendants of these Celts were identified as such 600 years later by the Christian missionary St. Jerome, who traveled through Galatia; to Jerome the language spoken there sounded like that of the Treveri, a Celtic tribe known to the Romans as the inhabitants of the Rhineland.

As they spread across Europe and into Asia, Celts of the La Tène period introduced, along with the new art style, technological improvements in their main occupations: warfare and farming.

Thus, after the rise of the La Tène culture, iron was used much more widely than in Hallstatt times. Carpenters worked with iron saws fitted into wooden frames, not unlike modern hacksaws, and they possessed a kind of rudimentary wood screw.

Some of these developments bore the stamp of outside influences, the result of increasing contacts with other civilizations, especially those of Greece and Rome. But like the derivative material in La Tène art, the new ideas were Celtized.

From their contacts with the people to the south, European Celts borrowed the idea of coins, imprinting them with symbols drawn from the repertoire of La Tène art. For the Classical heads of Greek and Roman coins, they substituted water birds, cult animals, sun symbols and the strange masklike faces that were a favorite Celtic design device. But these coins were mainly used in trade with foreign merchants. Among themselves, the Celts preferred to calculate the worth of an object in terms of commodities, especially the two commodities they traditionally valued most: cattle and slaves. So entrenched was the notion of slaves as units of value, in fact, that as late as the 12th Century, in Ireland, men measured the worth of a field or a chariot in terms of a cumal, or female slave. In the conversion table for this commodity system, one cumal equaled six heifers or three milk cows.

The chief source of slaves, of course, was conquest. Judging from the archeological evidence, the more the Celts prospered, the more they occupied themselves

A wheeled reaper, pushed by a mule
and attended by two workers—a driver
behind and another man to clear the
grain being cut by the reaper's teeth—
appears on a Second Century A.D.
relief found on a grave in Luxembourg.
The contrivance was invented by the
Celts, who passed it on to the Romans.

with raiding and warfare. Blacksmiths and chariot makers must have been constantly encouraged to outdo themselves in the production of ever more splendid weapons and equipment, and builders must have been constantly employed in enlarging and improving Celtic fortifications.

Driven by leather-coated charioteers, jolting over the rough roads that cut through the Celtic countryside, the two-wheeled Celtic war chariots, in particular, must have been a sight to behold. Their wickerwork bodies bore bronze fittings decorated with intricate designs, and their teams of fast ponies were decked in metal-studded harnesses as grand as those worn by 19th Century brewery horses. One Roman historian even reported seeing a Celtic war chariot entirely covered in silver, though that par-

ticular vehicle must have been intended purely for use in ceremonial functions.

As for the Celtic hill fort, it had now become a permanent dwelling place with some of the characteristics of a proper town. Along trade routes it often functioned as a marketing and manufacturing center that included not only the houses of noblemen and workshops of craftsmen, but also stalls and booths for farmers and traders to use when they entered the fortification to exchange wares and produce. In some places these communal centers of activity enclosed large areas and contained sizable permanent populations. Near Autun, France, one Celtic walled site covered an area of 335 acres and may have held as many as 300,000 people.

The Romans called these Celtic settlements oppi-

The rows of 80-foot-high earthworks that once bounded the Iron Age town of Maiden Castle in Dorset, England, are now a quiet grazing place for sheep. The town's population of around 5,000 people lived on the plateau at the upper right from about 300 B.C. to 70 A.D.

da, and archeologists have borrowed the term to distinguish them from the older, less sophisticated hill forts. At a site in Dorset, England, called Maiden Castle, excavations have uncovered evidence of successive waves of occupation that make it possible to trace Maiden Castle's development from a modest hill fort to an *oppidum* of 45 acres, elaborately protected by multiple ramparts. Maiden Castle rises from a hill in Dorset, novelist Thomas Hardy's country, and Hardy has described it in his typically gloomy style as "a stupendous ruin varied with protuberances, which from hereabouts have the animal aspect of warts, wens, knuckles and hips. It may indeed be likened to an enormous, many-limbed organism of an antediluvian time."

The hilltop site was occupied more or less continuously beginning about 2000 B.C., when the earliest group of occupants carved a series of intermittent ditches into the chalky earth. Celtic colonists began to use the site around 300 B.C., and they encircled an area of 16 acres with a continuous ditch 20 feet deep and 50 feet wide at the rim. All the material excavated from the ditch was hoisted in basketfuls to build a rampart at the top, twice the height of a man and 12 feet thick. A framework of timbering anchored the earth and chalk and held the rampart in place.

Piercing the rampart on opposite sides were two entrances lined with palisades, each apparently guarded by 14-foot-wide wooden gates. Causeways connected the two entrances with a wide, flat area beyond the ditch, and outside one entrance a wooden enclosure for sheep and cattle was put up in an area roughly the size of a football field. The surface of this corral, as well as that of the causeways, was

paved with flint, which had been rolled into the wet surface of the chalky soil to form a kind of cobbling. The paving was probably intended to keep the feet of the penned animals dry, curbing hoof diseases, and to prevent chariot wheels from getting stuck.

The interior of Maiden Castle contained small huts; their rectilinear, round and polygonal foundations are still there. The castle is also fairly honeycombed with barrel-shaped pits, some of them as large as 11 feet in diameter. From refuse found in the pits, archeologists think some of them were used for storage, drainage and garbage disposal. But others seem to have served as outdoor dining rooms.

Clustered around a fire at the bottom of the pit, protected from the penetrating Wessex winds and rain by some sort of roof, the Celtic inhabitants of the castle feasted on joints of pork and mutton and disposed of the bones by tossing them over their shoulders. When the litter on the dining-room floor got too deep for comfort, they simply spread over it a fresh layer of earth and chalk, and built a new campfire on top.

As time went on, the fortifications of Maiden Castle were extended. At the final stage of its occupancy in the First Century A.D., its ramparts were twice their original height and may have surrounded a population of as many as 5,000 people. In fact, the ruins at Maiden Castle contain a poignant record of how these Celts met their end: a single human vertebra pierced by a Roman arrowhead, which was probably shot from a Roman siege engine when the armies of the general Claudius overran Britain in 43 A.D.

That grisly memento essentially represents the end of a Celtic way of life carried on at Maiden Castle and hundreds of similar communities the length and breadth of Europe during a period of some eight centuries. It was a mode of existence that comes down to the present only as tantalizing fragments that raise many unanswered questions. But the few pieces that do fit together reveal a vivacious people driven by extraordinary energy.

Fine Art Fashioned by a Rough People

The complicated outlook of the Celts, with its emphasis on the magical and the supernatural, was most fully expressed in the craft of their metalsmiths, particularly in the art of the La Tène culture, which began around the mid-Fifth Century B.C. and continued on the Continent for some 400 years, and longer in the British Isles.

La Tène art, named for the Swiss region where the first examples of it were found, combines geometric motifs from earlier Celtic styles with themes derived from other peoples —particularly the Greeks and Etruscans, but also the Persians and other Easterners. However, the effect of La Tène art is much more ambiguous than that of the realistic decorations appearing on objects imported by the Celts. As in a dream, hints of human heads—among the most sacred Celtic subjects *(pages 103-111)*—emerge from stylized scrolls and spirals, lyre motifs, and palm-leaf or vine-tendril designs. The flowing decorations appear on their armaments *(right)* and on drinking vessels, body ornaments, horse trappings and chariots.

Almost 32 inches high and fashioned of hammered bronze decorated with inlaid disks of red glass, this shield from southern England was probably used ceremonially rather than in actual battle. Its whorls and bull's-eyes appear to be abstractions of the long, winding tendrils of vines.

Battle Regalia of Highborn Warriors

Celtic art in the La Tène culture mirrored the attitudes of a warrior aristocracy whose chieftains were expected to put their might on display. To this end, they encouraged their metalsmiths—who were believed to have magical powers—to do their finest work, which was then used ceremonially as symbols of rank.

La Tène smiths not only expanded indigenous themes but also borrowed from other cultures, and in the process developed their techniques so skillfully and creatively as to establish a mastery that is indisputably their own.

Thus the triangular belt hook or buckle (near right), with its schematic human figure and stylized birds, derives from older motifs that also emphasized linear shapes. But the belt hook includes an Eastern theme as well: a hero confronting two beasts. The central figure, however, is no longer a literal human form, and the beasts have become highly abstracted two-headed dragons.

The curlicue decoration on the military helmet (far right), the most elaborate Celtic headpiece yet discovered, is probably based on patterns from Italian art objects taken back across the Alps by invading Celts. The scabbard (below) reflects the complexity of the Celts' artistic vision: no two of its rhythmic scroll-forms are exactly the same.

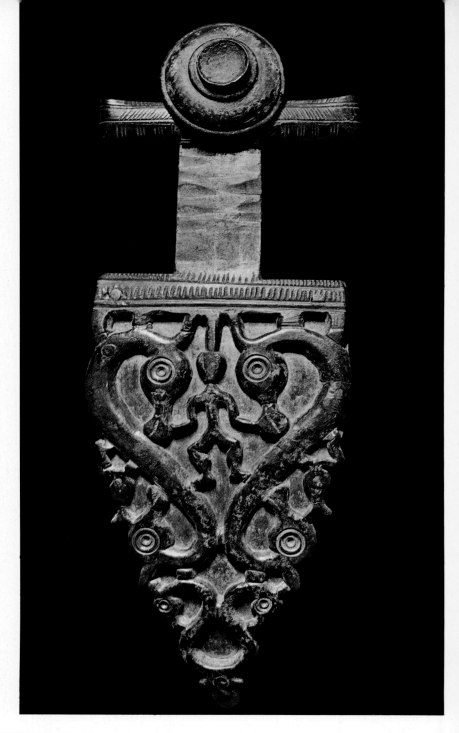

The bellicose dragons on this seven-inch-long belt clasp, unearthed at Hölzelsau in the Austrian Alps, recur as La Tène motifs. The beasts often show up on Celtic scabbards and belt fittings found south of the mountains.

This La Tène scabbard, from Bugthorpe in Yorkshire, England, is ornamented with an intricate scrollwork design on sheet bronze and ends

The Amfreville helmet—discovered in 1861 near the French town of that name—is made of bronze and iron and has a central gold band.

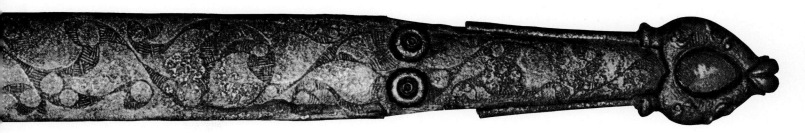

in a cast-bronze tip or chape (right). The 24-inch-long sheath holds the original iron sword-blade, so badly rusted that it cannot be removed.

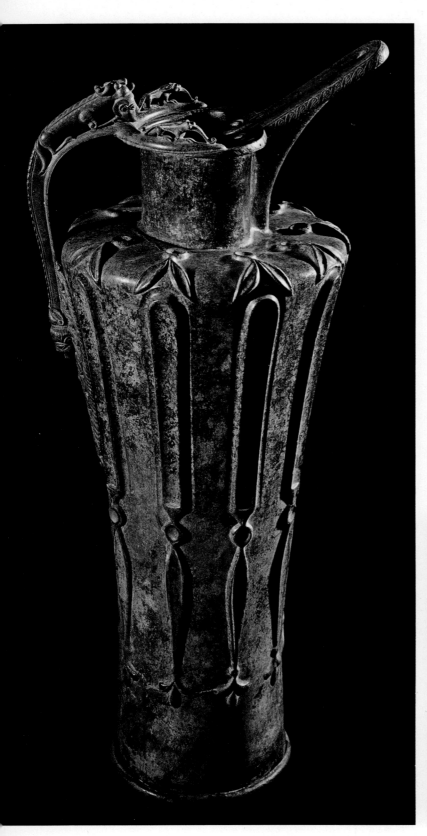

Elegant Vessels for Drinking

It has been said that Celtic art owes much to Celtic thirst. At the start of the La Tène period the Celts had for some time been trading with a Greek colony in what is today the port of Marseille —where they bought Greek wine. It came in large vessels decorated with Classical designs whose themes would have been familiar to the Celts, for whom feasting was an important event. Inevitably, La Tène metalsmiths soon created their own wine vessels, bearing vivid Celtic patterns.

One of the most ornate of these artifacts, the Dürrnberg flagon *(left)*, has on its handle a fearsome monster devouring a human head. A gold drinking horn *(right, top)* and a hammered sheet-gold casing for a bowl *(right, bottom)* are further testimony to the importance the Celts attached to the consumption of wine.

The beaked Dürrnberg flagon, nearly 19 inches high, unearthed in Austria, attests to the skill of Celtic craftsmen. Mounted on each side of the vessel's mouth is a long-tailed beast (detail, below) with what appears to be a human limb protruding from its gaping mouth.

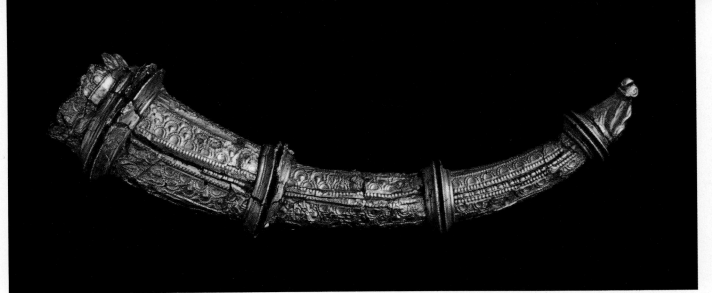

This drinking horn from Germany, measuring six inches along its outer curve, is gold with a bronze lining, fashioned on a matrix of oxhorn.

Discovered in a princely grave in a western region of Germany in 1849, the Schwarzenbach bowl, five inches in diameter, bears openwork gold designs based on Greek plant and leaf motifs.

Curling tendrils decorate the end of a gold torque found at Waldalgesheim, Germany. The ornament is almost eight inches in diameter.

Finery to Adorn Mortals and Gods

Torques, or neck rings, which the Celts copied from older European versions, were among the most characteristic ornaments worn by the Celts. Other items included bracelets, armlets (right) and rings. But apparently the torques indicated the social and religious status of the wearer.

Pliant, sometimes hinged so that they could be opened to encircle the neck, torques may also have been worn by women as head ornaments. Most of the valuable specimens made of gold and silver come from women's graves, suggesting that men, instead of burying their torques, usually passed them down to the sons in the family as an inheritance. Such a bequest may have signified the transfer of leadership in a family or tribe.

Discovered at the Tarn River in France, a bronze armlet nearly four inches in diameter is decorated in high relief and features familiar Celtic spirals. Unlike those of gold and silver, bronze jewelry was often sold to non-Celtic peoples.

The massive Trichtingen torque from Germany measures almost 12 inches around and weighs more than 13 pounds; decorated with the heads of bulls that are in turn wearing torques, the piece was probably a symbolic ornament for a religious sculpture.

Splendors for Horses on Parade

When the outstanding Celtic warriors put on displays of their power, they paid careful attention to the accouterments of their chariot ponies as well as to their weapons and persons. From a number of grave finds have come examples of such trappings as the evocative horse's face found at Melsonby in Yorkshire *(near right)* and a bronze harness disk from France *(far right)*.

As was true for all the more elaborate La Tène objects owned by warriors, these adornments were probably designed for parade rather than battle, reflecting a proud and boisterous love of show.

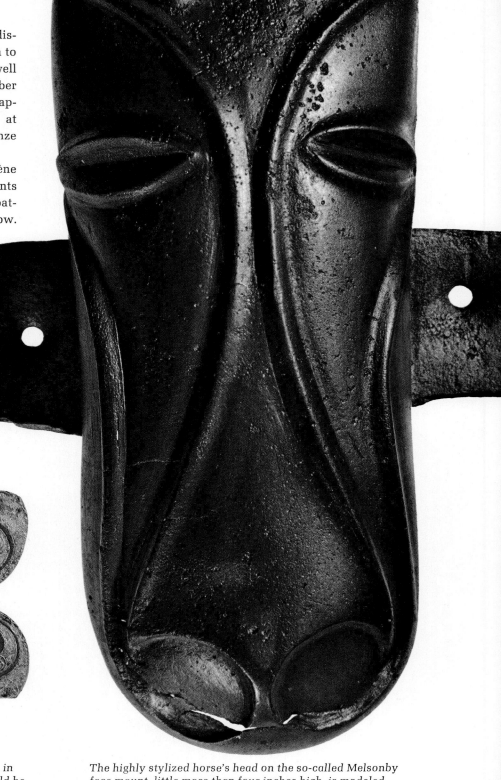

The First Century A.D. harness mount, from Santan in eastern England, measuring about three inches, could be attached to a strap and used to dress up a chariot horse.

The highly stylized horse's head on the so-called Melsonby face mount, little more than four inches high, is modeled in sheet bronze. It may once have been attached to a chariot.

A bronze harness disk, with a diameter of almost 10 inches, once ornamented a chariot found at Saint-Jean-sur-Tourbe in central France.

Suppose, like the dry bones Ezekiel brought together in the Old Testament to make the children of Israel, the bones of the Celts could also be reassembled. Covered with flesh and given breath "from the four winds," they would emerge from their tumuli looking just as they looked in their heyday, in the centuries before and immediately after the birth of Christ. What sort of people would they be? How would it be to confront them face to face? As they moved through the routine activities of their lives, what would be their human condition?

Nobody can be sure. The reports set down by Greek and Roman writers were obviously biased. Many of them viewed the Celts as quaint, unreliable tribes with dubious credentials for becoming fit associates for civilized men. The other principal source of information—and speculation—about the Celts lies in the myths of Ireland, which suffer from their own bias and share with all myths a strong leavening of fantasy and invention. But taken together, sources do create a vivid picture of the Celts that draws substantial support from archeological evidence.

To the urban Greeks and Romans who knew them as contemporaries, the Celts seemed little more than clusters of unworthy clans pursuing a hivelike existence. They were rural, seemingly without taste in food and dress, and lacking in manners and morals. Physically they seemed extraordinarily large, often

Mounted and wielding a spear, a Celtic nobleman gallops off with his hound in pursuit of a boar. The bronze tableau is set on a wagon slightly less than 10 inches long, fitted with movable wheels and bells that tinkle. Such assemblages of figures on wagons were important to the Celts in representing their divinities, but this 2,100-year-old artifact—with its sporting theme—could have been a sophisticated plaything.

alarmingly so. "Nearly all the Gauls are of a lofty stature . . . terrible from the sternness of their eyes," the Roman writer Ammianus Marcellinus reported to his countrymen in the Fourth Century A.D.

Almost to a man, the Greeks and Romans were struck by the Celts' pale skin, which flushed when they were angry, and by the masses of red-gold hair —an astonishing sight to the eyes of the "civilized" Mediterraneans. In 38 A.D., when the emperor Caligula planned to drag a group of Celtic captives through the streets of Rome, he ordered the hair of a few atypically brunet prisoners to be dyed red, giving them the distinct appearance of exotic animals. Beards were common among the Celts, and so were heavy, drooping mustaches that trapped food as they ate. Through these mustaches "drink passes, as it were, through a sort of strainer," wrote Diodorus, a fastidious Sicilian.

Before going into battle, the Celts habitually washed their hair in lime and pulled it back as it dried into stiff spikes, perhaps to keep the locks from falling in their eyes. At any rate, the lime gave them a frenzied, onrushing appearance that never failed to astonish their adversaries. (Perhaps the lime, which is a bleach, also helped to account for the Celts' red-gold hair color.)

If the Celtic men, as viewed by their more sophisticated contemporaries, appeared unrefined, the Celtic women seemed flamboyantly uninhibited. Though they twisted their long hair into braids, and sometimes piled it atop their heads in elaborate coiffures, they were generally too fond of ornaments. They moved to the constant sounds of tinkling necklaces and bracelets, and there were little bells sewn to the fringed ends of their tunics. Over the tunics went

gaudy cloaks patterned with bright-colored stripes and checks, and often elaborately decorated with embroidery of silver or gold.

The Celtic women were also described as preoccupied with make-up. They painted their fingernails, reddened their cheeks with *ruan*, an herb, and darkened their eyebrows with berry juice. But they were as warlike as their husbands—a trait one Roman warned his countrymen to beware. "A whole troop of foreigners would not be able to withstand a single Gaul if he called his wife to his assistance," admonished Ammianus Marcellinus. "Swelling her neck, gnashing her teeth and brandishing her sallow arms of enormous size, she begins to strike blows mingled with kicks as if they were so many missiles sent from the string of a catapult."

The Celts were also judged to be prodigious eaters and drinkers. The feast of one Celtic ruler, who invited his entire kingdom as well as any strangers passing through his domain, was said to include so much food and drink that the monarch built an enclosure a mile and a half square to serve them. The menu for this particular banquet was not recorded. But a typical Celtic meal was built around quantities of boiled pork, beef, ox, game and fish, along with honey, butter, cheese, curds and milk, wine, mead and beer. The diners could address themselves to this board for days on end without a break.

The setting for such a feast, normally at the home of a tribal chieftain, was a barracks-like building of wood, whose sole decoration was apt to be the carved and ornamented pillars that held up the roof. Usually the guests simply sat in a rough circle. But in the grander circumstances of a powerful noble's house, the dining hall was more elaborate: all around the perimeter of the building were cubicles, separated from each other by wickerwork partitions, and within these cubicles sat the noble guests, each with his own retainers. There were no chairs; the diners sat on animal pelts or rushes spread over the earthen

Skilled in the use of bronze tools, Celtic builders in 600 B.C. carefully shaped and fitted logs to create solid structures. A detail (right) from the Hallstatt blockhouse (left)—a site near Vienna where Iron Age buildings have been reconstructed—brings into sharp focus the precision of the construction methods. Rafters secured by leather thongs were covered with a thatch of straw and wheat. The thatched cone next to the house was originally a bakehouse, sunk partly into the ground in order to insulate it.

floor, and the tables were wooden boards resting on supports that lifted them just above floor level.

According to the Greek historian Athenaeus, a strict protocol was observed in the seating arrangement. The place of honor, in the center, was always occupied by the most illustrious guest: the bravest warrior, the highest ranking nobleman, the richest member of the tribe. Next to him sat the host; and on either side of the host and the guest of honor sat the other guests in order of diminishing importance. Some attendants, such as shield-bearers, stood during the meal; but spearmen, apparently enjoying higher status, were entitled to be seated—off to one side of their masters.

Servants moved among the guests bearing trenchers of food and flagons of wine, the drink of the upper classes. Lesser folk drank a wheaten beer mixed with honey called *corma*, and they often drank it from a common cup. Though Athenaeus observed that each man drank only a little at a time, "not more than a mouthful," he did add that "they do it rather frequently." Athenaeus also reported that, except for the occasional use of a dagger to cut a troublesome portion of meat, the Celts ate with their fingers. "They partake in a cleanly but leonine fashion, raising up whole limbs in both hands and biting off the meat."

While guests dined, minstrels played lyres and sang songs of tragic love affairs and heroes slain in combat. On occasion, the guests themselves provided some entertainment. "At dinner they are wont to be moved by chance remarks to wordy disputes," Diodorus reported. The disputes usually began as boasting matches but often ended in challenges to single combat, which took place immediately, before the assembled guests. Now and again these confrontations ended in the death of one of the duelists. Diodorus also said that when the diners had finished their meal and wanted to sleep, they simply stretched out on the ground "upon the skins of wild animals to wallow among their bedfellows on either side."

Occupying a prime location in most Hallstatt dwellings was a wooden loom with weights hanging from each of the vertical warp threads. One woman did the weaving for each family.

Made of sun-dried clay, the family's sleeping ledge was made comfortable and warm with furs. On the wall are clothes, spears, pots and a two-horned staff used in refereeing games.

When in peacetime the Celtic noblemen were not feasting, they spent their time hunting and playing games. They were especially fond of a board game called *fidchell*, which was rather like chess except that it was played with pegs. For younger men and boys the favorite game was hurley, or hurling, a field game on the order of hockey but played with a ball instead of a puck. In some princely games of hurley, the playing ball was said to be made of silver.

But idle pastimes were promptly put aside when it came to the Celts' main preoccupation: warfare. And it was in their role as warriors that the Celts most amazed their Mediterranean neighbors. The Greeks and Romans wrote repeatedly of the daring *gaesatae* —spearmen—who went into battle naked except for neck torques *(page 59)*, and of the frenzied behavior of ordinary Celtic soldiers, who worked themselves into a fury before going into battle and then fought wildly, like madmen.

In the aftermath of battle, they behaved in a fash-ion equally incomprehensible to the Greeks and Romans who were their adversaries. They rode from the field with the heads of their fallen enemies dangling from the necks of their horses. Later, the heads were nailed to the walls of their houses or were embalmed in cedar oil to be taken out and displayed proudly to visitors—although the cedar-oil treatment, according to Diodorus, was mainly reserved for the heads of distinguished enemies.

Naturally enough, for political reasons, the Greek and Roman writers tended to focus on the most sensational or unpleasant aspects of the Celtic character, including what they deemed a lack of sexual restraint. And yet the accounts often hint at another humor, suggesting that the Celts may not have been as uncivilized as they were painted. The finicky Diodorus may have found them barbaric for their habit of straining wine through their mustaches, but the Celts washed with soap—a custom the Greeks and Romans themselves had not yet adopted. Also, the

There was no designated baker in a Hallstatt village, so the bakehouse was used by everyone. First, fires were stoked to heat the domed clay ovens; then, when the flames subsided, dough was spread on pottery plates and placed inside. Baked goods not eaten immediately were left to harden, then broken up and boiled with water or milk into a kind of gruel. The planks hanging over each oven deflected heat and smoke toward a hole in the roof.

Celtic warrior, if he did not go to war naked, was truly fastidious in his insistence on donning a clean linen shirt before going into battle. And obesity was so repugnant to Celts that they meted out punishment for it. "They try not to become stout and fat-bellied," Strabo wrote, "and any young man who exceeds the standard length of the girdle is fined."

Neither were the Celts as rampantly licentious as their contemporaries pictured them to be. What the Greeks and Romans took for promiscuity was often no more than a difference in codes of social conduct. The Roman writer Dio Cassius, more fair-minded than most of his countrymen, quoted with relish the retort of one Celtic wife to the jeering charges of promiscuity leveled at her by a Roman matron. "We fulfill the demands of nature in a much better way than do you Roman women," said the Celtic lady acidly, "for we consort openly with the best men, whereas you let yourselves be debauched in secret by the vilest."

Beyond that, what often passed for Celtic promiscuity was simply the carefully controlled practice of polygamy. Though Celtic men—and sometimes Celtic women—were permitted to have more than one mate, the laws surrounding these relationships were infinitely and meticulously detailed. In fact, the Celts had an acute sense of the rights and duties, both familial and tribal, of every member of their society, from the humblest laborer on up to the king.

The rules governing this highly structured society were, of course, never written down; they were passed along orally by the Druids, who functioned as lawgivers as well as priests. But the general outlines of Celtic society can be grasped by reading between the lines of the Irish epics. Furthermore, many of the details of that social order are preserved in the ancient Irish law tracts, the so-called Brehon laws that governed Ireland in the centuries before Irish society was infiltrated by the legal system of the neighboring British.

A typical Celtic dwelling of 100 B.C., in the La Tène period, had a pitched roof of reed thatch that almost concealed walls of wattle and daub set deep in the ground and braced by wooden posts.

At the highest levels of Irish society were the kings, who were themselves arranged in grades of power. Each individual *tuath,* or tribe, had a king, but some of the tribal monarchs were strong enough to become, in addition, overlords of weaker tribes, and thus were called overkings. Above the overkings, with their petty empires, were four kings-over-kings, who were the rulers of Ireland's four provinces: Connaught, Ulster, Leinster and Munster. (In the old Irish tales these provinces were named, respectively, Connachta, Ulaid, Lagin and Mumu. There was a fifth and middle province too: Mide. Also known as Meath, it was absorbed by its neighbors after a brief existence. Its borders roughly correspond to those of modern County Meath in central Ireland.)

None of the kings in this royal chain of command enjoyed real sovereignty in the modern sense of the term; they did not make or unmake laws, nor did they judge or punish violators. In a primitive version of the doctrine of separation of powers, the king, at whatever level, was primarily concerned with the tribe's military business and with intertribal diplomacy. His subjects looked to him for military leadership in time of trouble, and in return promised him military service. Similarly, the king was entitled to an annual tribute from his subjects, and in return he gave them gifts of property, such as land or cattle. The benefits of this contractual arrangement were mutual: the king gained men-at-arms when he needed them and a substantial income; his subjects got the protection and prestige of being associated with a powerful ruler.

Kings were elected by their peers—other men of noble birth; but the king himself had to be a member of a royal family. Actually, this requirement did not limit the choice of rulers as much as might be assumed. Like every Celtic family, a royal family consisted of all the descendants of a single great-grandfather—a social unit that in four generations of polygamous marriage could field a considerable number of candidates. Given this many contenders, in fact, politics must have played an important role in the final selection of a king. And undoubtedly the politicking must sometimes have led to family arguments and even to bloodshed.

Whatever the election's outcome, however, the king-elect was always assumed to have earned his kingship through divine intervention. This is a very old tradition, common to most Indo-European societies, and in Irish society it was acknowledged in a variety of ways. In the Irish epics, young men frequently become kings by sleeping with ugly women who turn out to be deities. Queen Medb of Connaught, who appears in many of the ancient tales and takes credit for being the principal agent in the choice of no fewer than nine Irish kings, is often pictured as both divine and physically loathsome. In the same tradition, Lugaid, a legendary Irish hero, achieves kingship by sleeping with a hag. "I will tell you, gentle boy," she whispers softly into Lugaid's ear, "with me the high kings sleep. I am the graceful slender girl —the sovereignty of Scotland and Ireland." Lugaid accepts her offer, perhaps with qualms, and sure enough he becomes a king.

Rituals with religious overtones also played a part in the king's inauguration. Giraldus Cambrensis, a Welsh historian writing in the 12th Century, asserted that the king-elect of a Celtic tribe mated ritually with a white mare, after which the mare was slaughtered, cut in pieces and boiled—the king first bathing

Set against an interior wall of the La Tène dwelling are reconstructions of ancient Celtic wood and iron implements: sickles, a scythe, knives, woodcutters' axes, and pots. The durability and variety of such tools facilitated Iron Age man's harvesting and construction—as well as cooking—chores.

in the broth of this meat and then drinking it. "These unrighteous things being duly accomplished," Giraldus reported, "his royal authority and dominion are ratified."

Actually, for all Giraldus' disapproval, the ceremony he described may have been based on a very ancient religious ritual. In the scriptures of the Hindu religion—the Vedas—the wife of a ruler acts out a similar symbolic mating with a stallion or a bull; her purpose is to ensure prosperity and abundance for her husband's people through the union of man and the beasts of his fields. Perhaps the Celtic inauguration ceremony had the same ritual meaning.

Religion cemented the king's position after he came to office. And if he were deposed or assassinated, it was always for quasi-religious reasons, never for political ones: the king was assumed to have betrayed a sacred trust or in some way to have fallen from divine grace. A king was expected, for instance, to be a perfect physical specimen because, in effect, his person represented the health and well-being of the tribe. Thus in one tale a king named Nuada loses a hand in battle and quickly has another made of silver. The artificial hand is in every sense an exact replica of the real one, right down to the movable joints. Yet, unfortunately for Nuada, his people decide that he is blemished nonetheless and they require him to relinquish the kingship.

Immediately beneath the king in Celtic society were the tribal elite—the warriors, the learned men and, in some instances, the craftsmen. It is not clear who outranked whom at this level of society, which indeed had considerable fluidity—men rose and fell depending upon the king's favor and their own eco-

nomic fortunes. Probably the intellectuals constituted the group with the most stability, since people with special knowledge invariably commanded respect. Thus the Druids were honored as priests and lawgivers; the *filid*, or seers and satirists, were respected because satire was an important propaganda weapon against one's enemies; and the bards were rated highly as the tribe's historians. With their knowledge of poetry and music, the bards composed laudatory poems for their overlords that not only entertained them but also contained and perpetuated vital genealogical records.

The status of the craftsmen is less easy to fix. Their membership in the nobility must have been based on their expertise and their value to their patrons. Some blacksmiths, for instance, undoubtedly ranked high on the social scale, not only for their production of armaments but also for the overtones of magic associated with their craft; other smiths were regarded as little more than journeymen.

As for the warriors, though they shared the sporting life of the king—hunting birds with him, riding to hounds, pursuing wild boars from chariots—their status among the elite was probably the most insecure. Despite his noble lineage, each warrior's prestige depended upon his economic standing, and maintaining that standing involved risks.

Like the king, he owned property that he dispensed among "clients" in return for tribute rendered in the form of goods and services. But his rank was very much determined by the number of clients he could afford. A nobleman just below the king in social status could, for instance, have as many as 40 clients, while a lesser noble might have as few as 10.

This rare glass figure of a dog, only three quarters of an inch long, stands as a tribute to the skills of a First Century B.C. Celtic craftsman. Found in Walltertheim, Germany, the animal is fashioned of opaque blue glass on which the artisan fused ribbons of molten white and yellow glass.

In effect these clients were tenant farmers, but they were of two classes, "free" and "base." The free client—sometimes called a freeman—came from a higher social status than the base client and could technically be a base client's overlord. In the ancient legal tracts, a typical freeman possessed seven cows and a bull, seven pigs and a brood sow, seven sheep, a horse and enough grazing land to feed seven cows for a year. With three other farmers he owned quarter shares in a plow and plowshare, an ox, and a goad and halter; he also shared with the other three in the possession of a kiln, a mill and a barn.

A freeman's relation with his overlord was more advantageous than that of a base client: the free client's contractual obligation to the overlord ran for a fixed period of time and enabled him gradually to expand his holdings. For seven years the overlord rented him stock and received in return seven years of personal service within his household. The overlord also took a percentage of the freeman's annual income, paid in the form of finished goods rather than raw material: a freeman, in other words, paid his overlord in beer, say, rather than the barley used to make it. As interest rates go, the payments were exceedingly high—about one third of the freeman's annual output. But at the end of the seven years the rented stock became his to own, and the freeman was at liberty to enter into another contract—either with the same overlord, or with a different one if he chose to—for additional stock.

The base client's relation with his overlord, however, was more likely to be a dead end. Although he too received stock from his overlord in return for an annual payment of tribute, the stock did not pass permanently into his hands at the end of a fixed period.

Furthermore, his annual tribute was sometimes paid in the form of raw materials rather than finished goods. And unlike a freeman, whose service to the overlord was always performed within the lord's household, the base client was more like a field hand. He helped to bring in the harvest and did manual labor in the construction of forts.

In setting up a contractual arrangement between an overlord and a base client, there was also another important consideration. The overlord paid to the farmer a portion of his established honor price—literally the price of his honor. Under Celtic law every man had an economic value, pegged by the community to his standing in it. If the base client was injured while performing his obligations to the social unit, he was due compensation based on his honor price. Thus in paying an advance on his base client's honor price, an overlord was in effect buying a lien on his client's services; and in case of injury to the client, he could claim part of the compensation. The purchase of a base client's honor price more or less turned this class of farmer into a serf. Though technically he could detach himself from one overlord and serve another, merely by paying back the overlord's loan and the lien on his honor price, in fact the farmer was seldom in the economic position to do so. Usually he remained in permanent bondage.

Even so, base clients were still far better off than the men who stood at the very bottom of the Celtic social scale: the slaves. In this lowest stratum of society lived local undesirables and captives from other tribes—who were sometimes used as a medium of exchange; the price of a two-wheeled chariot might be reckoned as so many handmaidens. Surviving without land or family, the slave lived and died almost a total cipher, with hardly a pot to leave with his bones for scholarly rumination.

In this carefully structured Celtic world, with its emphasis on status and family, no man could operate outside the system, and allegiance to the system was vital. To ensure its continuity, the Celts—like many people before and since—attached special importance to the education of their children. The Celtic way was through fosterage, which in effect took children from their homes when they were quite young—before they had even reached the age of seven—and introduced them to the wider world of the tribe and the things the tribe would expect of them when they became adults.

The foster families were relatives and friends, selected on the basis of their social prestige as well as their economic standing. Sometimes no fee was involved, more often the father of the child reimbursed the foster parents in an amount commensurate with his own rank and with the child's sex: girls cost more than boys. For example, the expense of feeding, clothing and instructing a freeman's son was set at the value of six heifers or one and a half milk cows, while a girl's costs were pegged at eight heifers or two milk cows. Though a girl remained with her foster parents only until the age of 14 and a boy stayed three years longer, the cost of his education was lower because he ultimately helped to pay his way in service to his foster family and because he was deemed less troublesome to raise. A girl, in the Celtic view, was more fastidious and required more attendants, thus making her care more expensive.

Along with other children in the household, many of whom might also be foster children, each foster child learned the skills he or she would need later in life. A farmer's daughter learned how to grind grain and knead bread, for example, while a nobleman's daughter learned to sew and embroider. For boys the training always included basic physical activities: riding, swimming and using a slingshot. Noblemen's sons were, in addition, taught the skills associated with warfare: how to hurl a javelin, handle a sword and fight from a moving chariot.

In the Irish legends there are numerous allusions to the institution of fosterage, none more delightful than the story of the boyhood deeds of Cúchulainn, the hero of a cycle of tales in prose and poetry, the most famous of which is *Táin Bó Cuailnge,* or *The Cattle Raid of Cooley (pages 77-83).* The picture the tale paints of Celtic society in its basic respect for rules and integrity is a far cry from that presented in the writings of the Greeks and Romans.

Cúchulainn, according to a modern translation by Thomas Kinsella, pleads with his mother to let him join the 150 boys among the foster children attached to the household of King Conchobar of Ulster, who is his uncle and the greatest warrior in all Ireland.

Lively Performers for Celebrations

In 1861 French laborers digging in a sand quarry at Neuvy-en-Sullias, near the city of Orléans, chanced upon a cache of exquisite bronze statuettes that had lain buried for almost 2,000 years. Sacred treasures, they had been hurriedly hidden from marauding Romans. Included were vibrant figurines memorializing performers who enlivened Celtic holy celebrations by performing at temple feasts. The hoard also yielded the dignified figure of a male elder who may have been a holy man. The dates for these sculptures can only be placed approximately at 100 to 300 A.D., an era marked by the progressive decline of Celtic Gaul, as Roman legions fought bands of Gallic brigands and invading Germanic tribes.

A musician (left) in close-fitting breeches and a long shirt plays a now-missing instrument that might have been cymbals. The four-inch statuette's broken foot was never recovered.

Because this nine-inch figure suggests the imposing presence of a priest in the act of sermonizing, its subject may be a Druid performing a sacred rite.

Moving on her toes, a lithe dancer (right) swings through a ritual dance for which Celtic customs prescribed nudity. The six-inch figure is one of only three Celtic sculptures of dancers ever discovered—all of them near Orléans.

His body taut, a juggler (above) watches a ball tossed in the air to be caught in the cup atop his forehead. Scholars point to the five-inch figure and the others found with it as supreme examples of the Celts' skill at freezing action in metal.

The King is holding court at Emain, his capital, which lies about 30 miles from Cúchulainn's home on the Murtheimne Plain.

"You can't go," his mother said, "until there are some Ulster warriors to go with you."

"That is too long to wait," Cúchulainn said. "Point me out the way to Emain."

"Northward there," his mother said. "But it is a hard road."

"Still," said Cúchulainn, "I will try it."

So he set off with a toy shield made out of sticks and a toy javelin and his hurling stick and a ball. He kept tossing his javelin ahead and catching it again before it hit the ground.

Then he ran up to Conchobar's boys without getting them to pledge his safety. He didn't know that no one went out to them on their field of play without getting a promise of safety from them.

"It is plain this young fellow is from Ulster," said Follamain, Conchobar's son, "and yet he dares us."

They shouted at him, but still he came on against them. They flung three times fifty javelins at him, and he stopped them all on his shield of sticks. Then they drove all their hurling balls at him, and he stopped every ball on his breast. Then they threw their hurling sticks at him, three times fifty of them: he dodged so well that none of them touched him, except for a handful that he plucked down as they shot past.

At this point in the tale, Cúchulainn is overcome by Celtic rage—what the Romans called a *furor*. His hair stands on end; he squeezes one eye to a slit narrower than the eye of a needle and opens the other wider than the mouth of a goblet. He bares his teeth until his gullet shows, and he rushes the boys, laying low 50 before they flee through the gates of Emain.

Inside the walls, the troop of boys flies past King Conchobar, who is playing *fidchell*. Indeed, nine of them leap right over the *fidchell* board. Conchobar catches the pursuing Cúchulainn by the wrist as he darts past and brings him to a halt.

"These boys are being roughly handled," Conchobar said.

"I am in the right, friend Conchobar," Cúchulainn said. "I left my home, and my mother and father to join their games, and they treat me roughly."

"Whose son are you?" Conchobar said.

"I am a son of your sister Deichtine. I didn't expect to be hurt here."

"Well, why didn't you put yourself under the boys' protection?" Conchobar said.

"I know nothing about that," Cúchulainn said, "but I ask your protection against them now."

"You have it," Conchobar said.

With that, Cúchulainn turns away to chase through the house after the troop of boys.

"What are you going to do to them now?" Conchobar said.

"Offer them my protection," Cúchulainn said.

"Promise it here and now," Conchobar said.

"I promise," Cúchulainn said.

"Then," concludes the storyteller, "everyone went out to the play-field and the boys who had been struck down began to get up, with the help of their foster mothers and fathers."

Silver Panels and a Wild Celtic Tale

An intricately embossed silver cauldron *(right)*, unearthed in pieces from a peat bog at Gundestrup in Denmark's Jutland, has been identified since its discovery in 1891 as Celtic in origin. Many experts who have studied the bowl—now reassembled and housed in the Danish National Museum at Copenhagen—generally agree that the cauldron, 27 inches wide at the rim, dates from the First Century B.C. and was most likely brought as war booty from Central Europe to Denmark, where the ancient Jutlanders placed it in the bog, probably as a sacrificial offering.

The story told by the bowl's panels has remained largely an enigma. But recently a connection has been suggested between the Gundestrup cauldron's scenes and an Irish Celtic tale first written down in the Ninth Century A.D. According to one theory worked out at Harvard University's Peabody Museum, episodes in the Irish epic *Táin Bó Cuailnge (The Cattle Raid of Cooley)* parallel the story illustrated by the figures on the bowl.

The Harvard theorists believe that even though the names of people and places in the *Táin* are peculiar to Ireland, the appellations could have been adapted from those of another region, as was true of Greek myths that appeared in Rome. Thus the ancient Irish story would actually be a much older myth that originated—as did the bowl—on the Continent.

A dying bull is at the center of the Gundestrup cauldron (top). Some scholars suggest the animal represents the focus of a Celtic myth and that the panels inside the bowl illustrate the story. A face on an exterior panel (bottom) may be Medb, a goddess-queen in the Irish version of the tale.

The War Chariot of a Queen

Those scholars who theorize that the Gundestrup cauldron tells essentially the same story as the Christian-era manuscript versions of the *Táin* link the Irish epic with versions of the myth handed down from pagan times.

The Irish tale deals with Queen Medb, who was ruler of the region in the west of Ireland known today as Connaught. Medb invades northern Ireland in order to recapture a much-treasured brown bull named Donn Cuailnge. The animal once belonged to her, but has escaped and gone into King Conchobar's province of Ulster. Opposing Medb on Conchobar's behalf is a boastful young Ulster hero, Cúchulainn; he defeats the forces of Medb, led by her paramour, Fergus. But the bull—the original source of strife—dies following a fight of his own with a white-horned bull from Connaught named Finnbenauch.

According to Garrett S. Olmsted of Harvard's Department of Anthropology, the first of the Gundestrup bowl's five inner panels *(right)* could be a European variant of the opening scene in the *Táin* story: a queen in her chariot preparing to set off on an expedition to recover a bull.

Elephants protect the chariot-borne heroine in the cauldrons first panel. A menacing panther and two griffins (mythical animals with eagles' heads and lions' bodies), representing the goddess of war, prowl about her.

A Gallant Hero Beset with Foes

All the events recorded in the Irish *Táin*—including cattle raiding, the use of chariots and heroic bouts of bloody fighting—conform to the accounts of European Celtic society by Greek and Roman writers. Indeed, conducting warfare was the principal activity of the Celtic ruling classes.

If the panels on the Gundestrup cauldron do indeed deal essentially with myths that evolved into the *Táin*, the man in the horned helmet *(panel at right)* would correspond to the hero whom the Irish called Cúchulainn of Ulster; his adversary would be a counterpart of Fergus of Connaught; and the animals would be manifestations of the Celtic war goddess. In the *Táin*, Cúchulainn singlehandedly slaughters thousands of Queen Medb's warriors.

Pagan tales such as the *Táin* remained deeply rooted in popular belief well into Christian times. An Irish monk writing in the 12th Century bestowed "a blessing on everyone who will memorize the *Táin* faithfully," although, perhaps mindful of his sacred mission to reject paganism, he was quick to add a disclaimer: "Some things in it are devilish lies, and some are for the enjoyment of idiots."

Dodging griffins, two panthers and a venemous serpent, the hero wields a broken chariot wheel as he attacks his enemy. Cúchulainn, the Táin hero, had adventures like this one detailed on one of the cauldron's panels.

End of the Tale: A Brave Bull Dies

The ritual sacrifice of a bull, in many cultures the symbol of virility and strength, represents the climax of the story apparently embodied in the panels on the interior of the Gundestrup cauldron. The scene at right does not coincide exactly with the myth recounted in the *Táin,* in which the ancient Celtic version may have been adapted by the Christian monks who set it down in writing. Possibly the monks objected to such pagan goings on as ritual slaughter. Despite this editing, however, the *Táin* also ends with the death of a brown bull, and the final panel in the cauldron sequence corresponds closely to the last scenes of the *Táin.*

In the Irish version of the epic, the brown bull, called Donn Cuailnge, fights a battle with his rival, the white-horned Connaught bull. The Connaugtmen rush at the victorious Donn Cuailnge, threatening to kill him; but Fergus, Queen Medb's general, makes his men abandon their ideas of revenge and sets the bull free. Thus reprieved, Donn Cuailnge dashes joyfully about Ireland. On his way back to Ulster, he drops dead, exhausted by his exuberant victory celebrations.

The cauldron's final sequence features three bulls—the number had magical significance for the Celts—awaiting a sacrificial death. Surrounding each bull and his killer is a leaping feline beast, suggesting terror, and a racing dog.

One day during their conquest of Britain, Roman troops were terrified by a sight that met their gaze across the narrow Menai Strait separating Wales from the island of Anglesey. On the opposite shore an army of Britons was preparing for battle. According to the Roman historian Tacitus, women in black dashed madly among the warriors like Furies, their hair in disarray and flaming torches in their hands. Meanwhile a band of Druids, identifiable by their white robes, stood in the midst of this commotion "lifting up their hands to heaven and pouring forth horrible imprecations."

The Druids on this occasion were simply performing one of their various priestly functions: readying the Britons for battle by whipping them into a frenzy. But as Tacitus described it, the episode conveyed a kind of irrationality that was altogether unseemly to Roman eyes. Scenes involving the Druids described by other Classical writers reflected a similar bias. Diodorus, Strabo and Caesar, for instance, credited the Druids with being the architects and chief practitioners of a variety of unpleasant rites—one of which was human sacrifice. No wonder Tacitus, in concluding his account of the engagement at the Menai Strait, was relieved to be able to note that the Britons had been demolished "and their sacred groves dedicated to inhuman superstitions and barbarous rites destroyed."

Tacitus, however, was only a small boy when the

Sculpted in limestone, a monster animal symbolizing death squats on its hind legs, a human arm dangling from its mouth, its forepaws resting on two severed heads. The 43-inch-tall statue was discovered near Avignon, in southern France. The gruesome Third Century B.C. image may have served to inculcate fear in celebrants during the Celts' religious rituals.

incident at the Menai Strait took place; in spite of his vivid account, he had probably never even seen a Druid. There is also some doubt whether Diodorus, Strabo or Caesar spoke from actual experience. Many of the Classical world's opinions about the Druids were formed secondhand from reading the histories of the Greek writer Posidonius, who traveled through Gaul in the Second Century B.C., observed the Druids and wrote at length about his experiences. It was from Posidonius' factual accounts of certain Druidic practices (i.e., foretelling the future from the writhings of their sacrificial victims) that other writers derived their impressions of the Druids as a repugnant and sinister fraternity.

Yet the judgment of the Classical world was not unmixed. Diodorus himself once described the Druids as "philosophers and theologians." In the Second Century A.D. Greek scholars in Alexandria decided that the Druids, because they believed the soul was immortal, were actually great moral philosophers. The Alexandrians, comparing the Druids to Persian Magi and Indian Brahmins, deemed them to be religious men whose chief concerns were the study of nature and the contemplative enjoyment of a close relationship with the gods.

Certainly this idealized view of the Druids, like the opposite view derived from Posidonius, was also more speculation than fact. But unfortunately the Druids left nothing behind in writing, and so neither assessment could be confirmed or refuted. Indeed, conflicting ideas about the Druids have persisted right down to the present day. During the 16th Century, for instance, when translations of the Classical authors first became widely available in England and France, some people were embarrassed to discover such unsavory characters in their collective past, while others admiring the Druids' wisdom were happy to count them among their ancestors. One 16th Century English poet, Michael Drayton, rhapsodized over the Druids as "sacred bards, like whom great Nature's depths no man yet ever knew."

Not surprisingly, Drayton is little read nowadays, but since his time the Druids have appeared in many guises and many settings. They are stock characters in Gothic novels; they are subjects for garden statuary; and they have even been used in an opera —Vincenzo Bellini's *Norma.* In 1781 a London carpenter from Garlick Hill founded the Ancient Order of Druids, which gradually expanded and attracted many followers. One of them was the young Winston Churchill, who was initiated into the order in 1908 while still a student at Oxford. Dressed in the sheets and scarves believed to be correct Druidic apparel, members of the order met regularly—as some latter-day "Druids" still do—in such places as Stonehenge to conduct rites accompanied by eerie organ music. The order had a certain entertainment value, but its trappings were undeniably bogus.

There was nothing bogus, however, about the original Druids. They were entirely real and their role was extremely important; their influence in the Celtic world, which was probably both good and bad, was thoroughly pervasive. Caesar recognized that the Druids were largely responsible for the Celts' aggressiveness, and he felt, therefore, that they should be suppressed. Yet despite his animosity, Caesar provided many valuable details about the Druids.

He described them as an itinerant priesthood that moved from tribe to tribe, exempt from having to pay taxes or bear arms. Their membership, he said, was exclusive. Young men flocked to join their ranks, but only those of intellectual aptitude were accepted; often their numbers were drawn from the Celtic nobility. Although there is no evidence that the Druids were organized in a hierarchy, Caesar reported that they were presided over by a head Druid, the most honored man among them, and when he died, his successor normally was chosen by vote—but sometimes, Caesar said, the matter of succession was settled by a contest of arms.

The training of a Druid, as Caesar described it, was both rigorous and time-consuming. It lasted as long as 20 years and was conducted in secret places like caves or remote woodland clearings. During the course of study, the Druidical candidate was required to memorize immense stores of material about Celtic law, history and religion—usually in the form of verse. "They consider it improper to entrust their studies to writing," Caesar observed. Apparently the Druids mastered enough Greek—picked up no doubt from Mediterranean traders—to transcribe Celtic names onto statues. But otherwise they had little use for written language, fearing that if their special learning should fall into the wrong hands, their religion might be vulgarized and corrupted. Beyond this Caesar thought that the Druids favored oral learning for two reasons: "first, because they were unwilling that their system of training be bruited about among the common people, and second, because the student should rely on the written word and neglect the exercise of his memory."

This notion that certain kinds of knowledge were better preserved in the mind than in writing, was largely responsible for the Druids' obscurity. Indeed, were it not for the accounts of the Druids' Greek and

Roman contemporaries, and for the early Christian monks who transcribed some of their lore, the Druids would have been virtually forgotten. Nothing would be known about the important role they played as jurists, scientists and religious leaders. Even their name might have been lost.

It was the Greeks and Romans who first identified them, calling them variously *druidai, druides, drysidae* and *dryadae*. And Pliny the Elder, the Roman procurator in Gaul in the First Century A.D., suggested that the name might have derived from "oak tree." Pliny noted that the Greek word for oak was *drus,* and his etymology may or may not have been correct; but in many Indo-European languages *dru* does mean "strong," while *wid* and variants of it commonly mean "knowledge."

Certainly the Druids do seem to have been possessed of a knowledge of many things. Caesar said that in addition to their religious responsibilities, they were called upon to settle nearly all disputes, public or private. "They also pass judgment, and decide rewards and penalties in criminal and murder cases," he observed, "and in disputes concerning legacies and boundaries."

As jurists, Druids throughout the Celtic world probably administered a legal code similar to the one set forth in the old Irish law tracts and epic tales. The social order reflected there is a system contrived as much by the gods as by men, and supervised as closely by otherworldly powers as by earthly judges. One of the most important of the divinely ordained precepts is truthfulness, an ideal that pervades the ancient Irish texts. "Three things that are best for a prince during his reign are truth, mercy and silence; those that are worst for a king's honor are straying from the truth and adding to the false," says one traditional Irish folk tale. And in another legend a hero who inadvertently gives false evidence is punished for his accidental wrongdoing by an ominous event: his house begins to slide down a hill. Fortunately, a virtuous, truth-speaking king intervenes, and by giving the correct version of the evidence causes the house to come to a standstill.

In the course of describing the Druids as judges, Caesar said that they held court once a year in a place he called the land of the Carnutes, at a site that may have been near Chartres, in France. "All who have disputes," wrote Caesar, "come here from all sides and accept their decisions and judgments."

Often the Druids' judgments involved entire families, for under Celtic law, as spelled out in the old Irish tracts, all of a culprit's immediate relatives—not just the wrongdoer himself—could be held responsible for his misdeed. Thus a man who had allowed his cattle to trample his neighbor's fields might be ordered to turn over his own fields to his neighbor for the period of a full season. But the offender's family was responsible for seeing that the order was obeyed.

By holding the family legally responsible in a dispute, Celtic law brought tremendous pressure to bear upon wrongdoers. If they defaulted on the Druids' judgment, the whole family was disgraced—and the Celtic family comprised everyone descended through four generations from one great-grandfather.

This extended family must itself have presented many knotty inheritance problems. To begin with, the men in Celtic society were allowed to take several wives, and each spouse had different legal rights, and so by extension did her children. Beyond this, the chief wife and her offspring enjoyed privileges that

The Celtic Holy Men: Savages or Sages?

Even today evidence of the Celts' priests and seers is so scant that scholars, attempting to formulate a picture of the Druids, must rely on secondhand reports from Greek and Roman writers and on folklore. The earliest modern studies, from the 16th through the 19th centuries, developed two opposing viewpoints, and some authors *(as in the examples at right, top)* attempted to reconcile them: a "hard" image, stemming from a distaste for the Druids' pagan cruelty, and a "soft" one, based on a growing interest and pride in the Druids as Europe's ancestral sages.

In this 17th Century A.D. engraving, set in a forest glade scattered with decapitated corpses, an artist imagined a Druid holding a sacrificial knife and an attendant priestess beating upon a drum with human thigh bones. Such conceptions fueled popular attitudes that reviled all primitive men as brutal.

A sharply contrasting 17th Century view projected this admirable image of the Druid as a humble natural philosopher, dressed in monkish clothing. Many of the elements in the continuing misconceptions about the Druids trace to the imaginings of Renaissance scholars.

Adding to the general confusion about the Druids were the very free translations of such Classical texts as Julius Caesar's description of human sacrifices made by the Celts. They led to this fantasy: a huge wickerwork effigy filled by the Druids with living men and set afire.

The artist who painted this aquatint in 1815 represented a Druid as a pontifical sage and seer, equipping him with a costume that was a bizarre mixture of contemporary research and sheer invention: a Classical robe, a medieval belt, and a gorget and diadem whose designs were appropriate to pre-Celtic Bronze Age times. The puzzle of the Druids persists even today; a 20th Century attempt at reconstructing what the Druids actually wore (pages 28-29) is, at best, only an educated guess.

did not extend to other members of the family. But if she produced no children (which was often the reason for a man's taking other wives), her inheritance rights might pass to the children of the subordinate wives. Furthermore, if the husband divorced his first wife—a step that could be accomplished by simply returning her to her family—then the question of inheritance among the remaining wives and children must have taxed even the Druids' profound wisdom. But the complexity of Druidical law may have been intentional—the purpose being to keep the administration of justice the Druids' exclusive province.

Besides involving whole families in legal judgments, Celtic law had other means for discouraging potential wrongdoers. One of these was the institution of suretyship. When a man had committed an infraction, he was fined according to his economic status, and he was obliged to provide guarantees of his ability to pay. These guarantees were supplied by a surety, a man of equal or higher station who in effect underwrote the defendant and agreed to assume the debt if he defaulted. But if this happened, the surety had the right to seize property from the offender, thereby inflicting serious economic hardship.

Sometimes, of course, neither family pressure, sureties nor fines were sufficient to enforce the laws administered by the Druids. This was especially true when the offender was of a higher social rank than the plaintiff, and therefore felt free to ignore the Druids' decision. In such cases the plaintiff had one last, curious expedient: from sunrise to sunset he could post himself outside the offender's door and refuse to eat until the debt owed him was paid. By custom the wrongdoer was required to fast, too, on pain of losing his honor—and no proud Celt would willingly dishonor himself before a member of a lower class.

Finally, when all else failed, the Celts could seek to enforce a ruling by appealing to the Druids to exert religious pressure: the holy men could exclude the transgressor from his tribe's sacred ceremonies. Though such ostracism could scarcely have given the plaintiff much satisfaction—for the debt remained unpaid—its consequences for the transgressor were alarming in the extreme. To be barred from tribal ritual in effect placed a man beyond the pale of the community. Nothing could be more serious, and only a stubbornly defiant man would risk such a penalty.

Just as Celtic law was rooted in the notion of a divine order and was made and enforced by a priestly panel of jurists, so Celtic science was based in religion, and the Druids were its chief practitioners. As scientists, the Druids were mainly concerned with astronomy. They studied the shifting relationships of the sun, the moon and the stars, and they used these cosmic changes to anticipate the future of earthly events. And for this purpose they invented a remarkably sophisticated calendar.

In 1897, in a vineyard in what is now the French town of Coligny, archeologists found the shattered physical remains of one version of this calendar. Pieced together, the Coligny calendar forms a bronze plaque about 60 inches high and 42 inches wide, and it dates from the late First Century B.C. The notations are in Roman letters and numerals, but the calendrical system itself clearly preceded the Roman occupation of Gaul and owed no debt to the Julian calendar invented by the Romans. The Coligny calendar divides the year into a system of months and seasons that coincides with the Celtic seasonal festivals—and clearly its makers and users were Celts.

The Celts reckoned time by nights instead of days. Fifteen nights made up what they called the bright half of the month (the period of the waxing moon), and 15 nights the dark half (the period of the moon's waning). The bright half was the auspicious time for doing things; the dark half held gloomier prospects. The Coligny calendar contains 62 of these lunar months plus two intercalary months. The Celts apparently adjusted their lunar year to the solar year by inserting an intercalary 30-day month alternately at two-and-a-half-year and three-year intervals. (The Julian calendar and its derivative, the modified Gregorian calendar now in use, accomplish approximately the same end by varying the lengths of months and by adding leap years.)

The Celtic year was divided into four seasons, each of which was ushered in by a festival period. While the laity celebrated with feasting and games, the Druids attended to the sober duties of honoring the gods with sacrifices—some of them animals and others, occasionally, humans. The purpose of the Coligny calendar was in fact to schedule these sacred events rather than simply to mark the passage of time.

The first festival of the Celtic year fell on the day that is February 1 on the modern Gregorian calendar. The festival was called Imbolc and it was apparently connected with the time when spring lambs were born and ewes came into milk. Little is known about the ceremonies of Imbolc, but its patron deity was the goddess of flocks and of fertility in general. She was called Brigit, or Brigid in Ireland, and Brigantia in England and on the Continent.

May 1, the second festival in the Celtic year, honored the Druids themselves and was also associated

Fashioned of six separate pieces of bronze during the First Century B.C., this 16-inch figure was dredged up from the Juine River in France in 1945. Its crossed legs, disproportionately small for the torso, terminate in deerlike hooves, indicating that the subject was a divinity.

Standing a little over five inches high, a bronze statuette found in France betrays a strong Roman influence in the realistic modeling of the body. But the trappings—a sun wheel, a thunderbolt and a spiral of lightning—identify it unmistakably as the Celtic god Taranis, called the Thunderer.

with fertility—mainly of newly planted crops and of cattle just put out to graze on green pastures. It was called Beltaine and its patron god was Belenos, a very ancient Celtic god whose name is inscribed on coins, wall frescoes and the pages of literary texts throughout southern France and northern Italy. His name is often connected with fire, and during the feast of Beltaine, the Druids conducted rituals that involved driving cattle through bonfires in what were apparently ceremonies of purification (page 28).

Lugnasa, the third festival of the Celtic year, began in mid-July and ended in mid-August, but its high point was a feast on August 1. Essentially Lugnasa was a harvest festival, and like the May Day celebration, its patron was Belenos. But in midsummer the god bore another name: in Ireland he was called Lug; in Gaul, Lugus; and in Wales, Lleu. According to Irish legend, Lug established the festival to honor his foster mother, who died on August 1 at the old Celtic stronghold of Lugudunum in France.

The fourth and last sacred celebration of the Celtic year actually marked the new year's beginning, November 1. The festival occurred on the preceding night, October 31, and it was called Samain. Perhaps the most important of the Celtic festivals, it was certainly the most solemn, for it commemorated the creation of the world when chaos was transformed into order. On Samain night the spirits of the dead were believed to return from their dwelling place to roam through the land of the living. It was considered a time of great danger. Although the spirits were at large for only one night, they could—if not properly placated with suitable sacrifices—continue to affect human affairs long after they had vanished. Samain and its mood of witchery and fear survive, of course, in the traditional observances of Halloween.

From the celebration of Samain, it is evident that the Celts felt that the real and the supernatural existed in close proximity to each other. Like country folk in some remote rural areas today, the Celts probably believed in witches and demons and other supernatural beings, and must have encountered them often in the dark and lonely byways. Propitiatory rites would have been demanded by these powerful forces—rites conducted by the Druids.

The religious responsibilities of the Druids may have been complicated by the number of deities they served. Like the ancient peoples of Mesopotamia and Egypt and like many people in Asia today, the Celts lacked a supreme god who, on occasion, addressed himself directly to man. The Celts' supernatural realm was crowded with a multitude of gods, most of whom had to be approached indirectly, and not by common men but by specialists: the Druids. They, and they alone, dealt with otherworldly powers. Altogether at least 400 different deities have been identified by modern scholars—partly through inscriptions on altars, partly through ancient Irish literature. Many of them are undoubtedly duplicates of one another, tribal gods whose names may differ from place to place but whose attributes and general functions are similar.

In contrast to the remote gods whom only the Druids could approach, there was an all-purpose deity in charge of each tribe's welfare. Every member of the tribe could communicate with him directly on a variety of important matters. He saw to it that oats germinated, that cows calved and that warriors won their engagements. In Ireland his name was Donn the Dark or Dagda the Good; in France he was called Su-

cellus, the Good Striker, and carried a long-handled mallet as a symbol of his might. His mate was an earth goddess, and the results of their union were all the tribal earthlings.

Besides this tribal god were deities with special functions, the best known of whom was Lug—the central object of the midsummer Lugnasa festival. Always portrayed as young, handsome and in command of unlimited talents, he invented games and horsemanship and was a sure shot with a sling or spear. Lug was a god of war, of manual arts, of journeys, of moneymaking and of commerce. In short, he was a god who oversaw all sorts of ambitious human undertakings. He was recognized and universally hailed throughout the Celtic world, and echoes of his name still survive in the names of such modern cities as Lyons and Laon in France, Leiden in Holland and Liegnitz in Poland.

Other Celtic deities who were worshiped under various appellations in various places included an antlered god, a blacksmith god and a god of oratory. The antlered god was often shown with a stag, a boar or a bull, and sometimes with a serpent as well—all symbols of fertility. He is thought to have been a god of domesticated herds or of the animal kingdom in general. The blacksmith god, who went by at least 15 different names, was associated not only with iron but also with thermal springs—and by extension with the curing of sickness. About the god of oratory little is known, but one Roman writer reported seeing him pictured as an old man with golden chains emerging from his mouth; the chains were attached to the ears of a group of eager listeners.

The goddesses in the Celtic pantheon were usually mother-goddesses with domestic attributes. They are shown holding infants or fruit or loaves of bread, but they were not always gentle; in Irish legend they could be vengeful when crossed. In some cases they operated alone, without consorts, and supervised some very manly pursuits. In Ireland two female deities, Scáthach and Aife, ran a kind of military school where Cúchulainn and other heroes went for training in the arts of combat. Mother-goddesses often appeared in groups of three—a significant number in the Celts' mystical world—as on the Romano-Celtic relief from Gloucestershire, England (page 95).

Like the antlered god, many deities were accompanied by animals or birds, with whom they were identified—and who sometimes appeared in the gods' stead. Dogs and wolves were common companions to deities. Another frequent animal symbol was a winged horse, which may have been the alter ego for a horse goddess called Epona. The boar, a great favorite of Celtic hunters and trenchermen, was apparently a divinity as well. And there is also a bull god, shown with a set of three horns.

Birds of every kind winged their way through the Celts' divine world, some of them benign, some malicious. Water birds—ducks, cranes, geese, swans, herons—were frequent stand-ins for both benevolent and mischievous gods or goddesses. In fact, the swan, which stood for purity, was a favorite disguise for gods in Irish legends who wished to pursue innocent maidens without alarming them. The raven, on the other hand, was the companion of goddesses of war, and the appearance of one of these black scavengers was considered a bad omen. Indeed, birds were generally thought to be bearers of divine information, and their calls and flight patterns were commonly interpreted by the Druids for insights into the future.

In addressing themselves to these deities and cult objects the Druids used rites that have sometimes been hinted at by the Classical chroniclers but never really explained. The Roman procurator Pliny, for example, reported witnessing a Druid ceremony that was carried out at the base of an oak tree. The tree stood within a grove, a kind of natural sanctuary, and it contained a rare growth of mistletoe. On the sixth day of the waxing moon, Pliny said, a Druid climbed the tree, and using a golden sickle cut off a sprig of mistletoe, dropping it into a white cloth held by two assistants. Whereupon two white bulls were sacrificed to a watching deity.

Pliny failed to say who the attending god was, and he does not seem to have known the purpose of the Druid ceremony under the sacred tree. And Caesar, referring to the Druids' practice of sacrificing human victims, does not even suggest to his readers what the purpose of the sacrifices was. Perhaps he introduced the subject merely to help justify his campaign against the Celts, intending to horrify the Romans and thus gain their support—although as late as the Third Century B.C., the Romans themselves were still sacrificing victims to propitiate their god of war.

Whatever the Druids may have hoped to accomplish with their mysterious rites, it is clear from archeological evidence that certain kinds of places were deemed more suitable for ceremonies than others. Springs and bodies of water, for instance, were favorite places for worship. Apparently there was a mystical appeal in the image of water emerging from the earth or emptying from a river or stream into a lake; the famous votive site at La Tène is just one example of the Celts' characteristic water sanctuaries. A site in northwestern France, among the streams

Drawing their divine powers from the earth, three mother-goddesses hold trays of bread and fruit as symbols of fertility. Found at Cirencester in England, the 31-inch figures in this stone relief reflect the Celtic belief in the threefold nature of divinity.

that feed the River Seine, yielded a cache of figurines *(pages 96-97)* dedicated to Sequana, the goddess of healing, indicating that divine powers were associated with this watery place too.

Hilltops and clearings within groves of trees were also locations for ceremonial rites. In fact, the Celtic word for sacred grove, *nemeton*, became a part of many European place names—such as Medionemeton in Scotland, Nemetodurum in France (now called Nanterre) and Nemetobriga in Spain—identifying those towns as former Celtic shrines.

The Roman poet Lucan described one particular sacred grove discovered by Caesar near Massilia (Marseille) in 49 B.C. and destroyed by him. It was a place "into which the sun never shone, but where an abundance of water spouted from dark springs. . . . The barbaric gods worshiped here and had their altars heaped with hideous offerings, and every tree was sprinkled with human blood." The images of the gods found in the grove were, said Lucan, "stark gloomy blocks of unworked timber, rotten with age," and superstitious natives of the area believed that the place was haunted. "The ground often shook, groans rose from hidden caverns below, yews were uprooted and miraculously replanted, and sometimes serpents coiled around the oaks, which blazed but did not burn."

A frightening world. And while there are few hints as to what transpired at the rites to propitiate these deities and cult objects, it is possible to perceive their general tenor and to picture a company of fierce Celts, now subdued and apprehensive, assembling in a clearing or crude temple carrying gifts and laying them before a sacred image.

The Druid's mysterious rites did not take place ex-

Votive Gifts for a Divine Healer

The spring that gives rise to France's River Seine was once the sanctuary of Sequana, a Celtic goddess believed to possess powers of healing. Her shrine was the region surrounding the river's source, northwest of the modern city of Dijon, and she gave her name to the people who lived there, the Sequani. In time, the river itself took on part of her name.

Perhaps because they issued forth as if by magic from the earth, springs were often sacred places for the Celts. Pilgrims by the hundreds traveled to the source of the Seine to present tributes and offerings to Sequana, either to appeal for her aid or to give thanks for her benevolence. There they deposited symbols of their ailing parts —such as the leg or organs at the far right. And to show appreciation for renewed health, the pilgrims brought likenesses of themselves.

Some 2,000 of these votive objects carved in wood, bronze and stone were uncovered in the last century in a marshy region near the Sequana spring. The area where the objects were found may have been a ritual bathing pool constructed during a phase of the sanctuary's expansion. In the water-logged soil, the wooden sculptures were preserved almost as effectively as the stone ones. All the objects were probably deposited there during the First Century A.D.

Dressed in a long, square-necked gown, this 34-inch woman of oakwood presents a serene expression that conveys gratitude for her good health.

A pilgrim in limestone, 23 inches high and clad in a long tunic, cradles a dog in her arms, perhaps ready to offer it in thanks to the goddess Sequana.

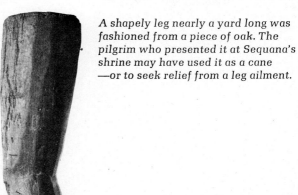

A shapely leg nearly a yard long was fashioned from a piece of oak. The pilgrim who presented it at Sequana's shrine may have used it as a cane —or to seek relief from a leg ailment.

Standing 18 inches tall, a man carved in oak peers out from beneath his hood. His pigeon-toed stance represents a handicap he sought to have corrected.

Three visages carved from a 27-inch log were probably mass-produced offerings. The maker could separate them for sale to several suppliants.

Representing a pharynx, lungs and abdomen, this wooden plaque 16 inches high must have been a gift from a sufferer of some grave internal illness.

clusively out-of-doors. In the 1940s while London's Heathrow airport was being built, construction workers stumbled upon the remains of a Celtic settlement dating from about 300 B.C. Among its several buildings, identified by rows of postholes, was one that stood well apart from the rest. It measured 18 by 15 feet and was surrounded by a second rectangle of postholes, 30 by 36 feet, forming a sort of colonnade. Conceivably this structure could have been a nobleman's house or a granary. But its rectangle-within-a-rectangle design is strongly reminiscent of a Greek temple, and scholars think it may in fact have been a kind of rustic Parthenon. At other Celtic sites in Britain, archeologists have found similar arrangements of double rows of postholes, with deposits of gold and silver artifacts as well as the skeletal remains of humans and animals, buried in a way that suggests sacrificial offerings.

Celtic temples have also turned up on the Continent. They vary in size, are sometimes round instead of rectangular and on occasion contain unmistakable evidence of their ritual function. At Holzhausen, in Bavaria, archeologists have unearthed the remains of what was once a wooden edifice 300 feet in diameter. Its walls enclosed three shafts, eight feet across and as deep as 120 feet (page 101). At first glance the shafts looked like wells but actually they were sacrificial pits. At the bottom of one a wooden stake was discovered, to which a sacrificial victim apparently had been tied. Surrounding the stake was a mass of organic material that on analysis proved to be remains of human flesh and blood.

As the Celts grew more affluent and became better acquainted with the Classical world, their temples became more grand and took on many of the architec- tural features of Greek and Roman temples. A few of these quasi-Classical temples were built of stone rather than wood and were decorated with paintings and bas-reliefs in the Classical style. At Entremont, in Provence, the approach to one Celtic temple was actually lined with statues of heroes—much in the manner of the avenue leading to a Roman villa.

What is most intriguing about the Entremont site, however, is its gallery of carved stone heads—heads of children, of curly-haired men, of veiled women. Most of the heads are fairly realistic in style, but those on one column—left from an earlier version of the Entremont temple—are strange masklike affairs, done as a cartoonist might do them. The eyebrows and noses are indicated only by lines, and the mouths are nonexistent. Probably these strange carvings are cult objects; but this hardly resolves the most baffling question of all: Why did the Celts venerate the human head with such passion?

The evidence of this veneration can be found wherever the Celts are found, but the search for answers to enigmas now takes a turn. Human heads, sometimes of a more grisly character than those of stone, keep appearing in excavations all around Europe. At Roquepertuse, near the mouth of the Rhône, archeologists discovered the ruins of a Celtic sanctuary that must surely have been one of man's more macabre places of worship. A flight of five steps leads up to three Classical pillars in which there are five niches. But the contents of the niches were decidedly unclassical. Apparently they held human heads, for the skull of one is still there.

No one living today can be certain what the human head meant to the Celts. The metaphysics of a people far removed in time and experience are usu-

This splendid, nearly life-sized boar, made of sheet bronze
during the First Century B.C., represents one of the most
important creatures in Celtic cult worship. Pigs were objects
of fear and reverence because it was believed that they
had been introduced to mankind by the gods and that in some
cases they were metamorphosed human beings. A certain
invincibility was also attached to them: Irish legend tells of a
boar who killed 50 hounds and 50 warriors in a single day.

ally impossible to plumb. Still, some scholars have tried. According to Anne Ross, an eminent British authority on the Celts, the head summed up their religious feelings in much the same way that the cross summarizes Christianity. The Celts, she says, probably considered the head the home of the soul, the essence of being, with connotations of immortality and even of divinity. Severed, it continued to retain a life of its own with power to achieve certain effects for its possessors.

In Welsh legend there is the example of a hero whose head lives on after his death to bring joy to his survivors. The hero's name is Bran the Blessed, and he loses his life in a fierce battle with an Irish king. As he lies dying, Bran orders the seven survivors of his army to cut off his head and carry it with them. They take the head with them to the other world and live there happily as Bran's guests for fourscore years. But the tranquillity comes to a sudden end when one of the seven disobeys an order, and they find themselves back on earth. Yet they still possess Bran's head and, in accordance with Bran's instructions, they bury it under London where it will purportedly guard Britain against evil forevermore. And so it might have done had not some unnamed culprit at a later point in the story dug it up—presumably to possess its magic.

So great was the Celts' belief in the potency of the human head that they managed to incorporate it into just about every artifact they put a hand to. Probably there has never been a symbol used more widely or for a longer time. Carved, painted or impressed upon stone, metal and wood, it looked out unblinkingly on the Celtic world from the surface of tiles, pots, neck torques, sword hilts, coins, cauldrons, bucket han-

dles and chariot fittings. And though the Druids must have supervised its use to some extent, they do not seem to have standardized its design. Sometimes it is featureless or nearly so; sometimes it has pop-eyes or eyes with multiple pupils; sometimes it is crowned with an elaborate headdress. There are Janus heads, facing fore and aft, and even a kind of Celtic trinity, a head with three faces, each looking in a different direction (pages 106-107).

Real heads—the heads of heroes or prisoners of war—were cut off and taken home to be nailed over doorways, or impaled on stakes around a victor's house; nails and stakes bearing the evidence of such use have been found at Celtic excavations. In one Celtic tribe, the Boii of the Po Valley, it was the custom to decorate prized skulls with gold and use them as drinking vessels—or so the Roman historian Livy reported. And Diodorus, commenting on the Celtic practice of preserving trophy heads in cedar chests, added that the people who owned these treasures could not be persuaded to part with them for their weight in gold.

Perhaps this cult of the disembodied human head helps explain why the Celts went into battle with such reckless courage, professing to fear nothing except the falling of the sky. And their bravado was certainly augmented by the Druids, who preached that death was not the end of life but a passage from one life to another, superior existence.

The Celtic heaven was like the earthly world, only far better. It was a land without sickness, calamity or old age, where all people were beautiful, especially the women. The sun always shone, birds always sang and no one wanted for food or drink, which appeared in abundance as if by magic. In the

Ritual Shafts with Divine Offerings

Because they believed that some of their gods lived inside the earth, the Celts bored deep holes in the ground and filled them with votive offerings to propitiate the underworld spirits. No one can be sure how these ritual shafts were dug —some are as deep as 100 feet—but they puncture the land in every region occupied by the Celts.

Many of the shafts, such as those diagramed at right, have been discovered in clusters, suggesting that they were centers of consecrated areas where the Celts came to worship.

These two examples, constructed more than 2,000 years ago, were found along with 30 others in an area about a mile square in the Vendée region of France. The one on the left was carefully filled in four distinct zones, which were separated by layers of stone. In contrast, the contents of the other shaft apparently were deposited in a haphazard fashion. Both of these pits contained similar objects: whole and broken pottery, human bones as well as those of deer, cows, pigs, dogs and foxes. The left shaft also contained a 20-inch wooden figurine of a female deity, along with pieces of deer antler. The other one yielded a 12-foot cypress trunk and a hollow oak log filled with bones, reflecting the Celtic belief in the sacredness of trees.

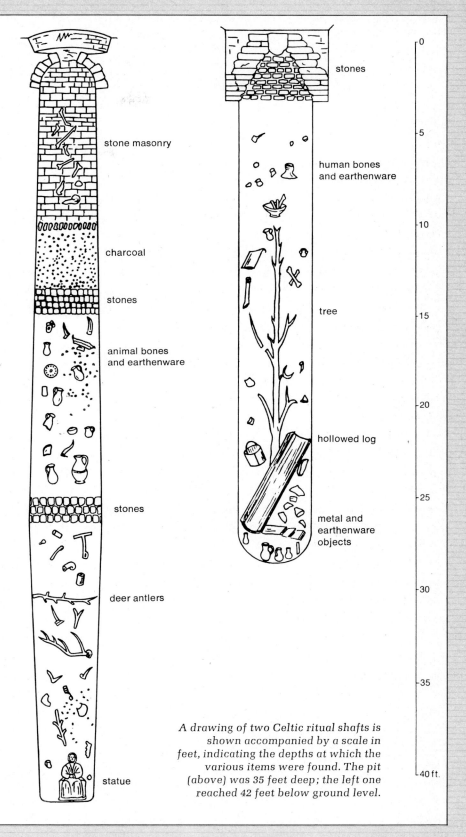

stone masonry

charcoal

stones

animal bones and earthenware

stones

deer antlers

statue

stones

human bones and earthenware

tree

hollowed log

metal and earthenware objects

A drawing of two Celtic ritual shafts is shown accompanied by a scale in feet, indicating the depths at which the various items were found. The pit (above) was 35 feet deep; the left one reached 42 feet below ground level.

ancient Irish legends, goddesses often invite heroes to join them there; one enticing deity calls it *Tir inna m Beo*, the Land of the Living. The Celts' hereafter was perhaps most rhapsodically evoked in these stanzas by an anonymous Irish poet, who referred to the heavenly abode as *Magh Már* (literally, Great Plain) and *Tir Már* (Great Land):

There, there, is neither "mine" nor "thine,"
White are teeth there, dark the brow,
A delight of the eye the array of our hosts,
Every cheek there is of the hue of the foxglove.

Purple the surface of every plain,
A marvel of beauty the blackbird's eggs;
Though the Plain of Fál be fair to see,
'Tis desolate once you have known Magh Már.

Fine though you think the ale of Ireland,
More exhilarating still is the ale of Tir Már.
A wondrous land is the land I tell of,
Youth does not give way to age there.

Sweet warm streams flow through the land,
The choice of mead and wine.
Splendid people without blemish,
Conception without sin, without lust.

In preaching such a heaven, the Druids made the Celts formidable adversaries in war, for death became an alluring prospect. Little wonder Caesar especially singled out their sanctuaries for destruction. So long as the Druids existed, he argued, they were a threat to Rome. Caesar claimed to be wiping out a "barbarous and inhuman" religion, but in fact he was probably more bent upon undermining the Druids' hold on their followers. Traveling among the Celtic tribes, administering their laws, interceding with their deities and stirring their hearts to war, the Druids inspired a dauntless people who might have become an invincible political unit. If the Druids had extended their influence, and had encouraged the Celts to act together as a political unit, Caesar's armies might have been stopped—and the history of Europe might have been very different.

The Bizarre Cult of the Severed Head

Human heads—actual skulls or representations of them in various art forms—were a persistent theme in Celtic life. Like the sign of the cross among Christians, the head was a symbol of the religious outlook of the Celts; they believed it was the essence of being and imbued with supernatural powers. And so the motif recurs in Celtic sculpture on masks and vessels and personal ornaments, created from every sort of substance—stone or clay or metal, carved or molded.

The Celts held that a human head could remain alive after the death of the body and that a severed head could keep evil away from home or fortress while ensuring good luck and success to its possessor. Victorious Celts gathered the heads of their enemies after battle and displayed them —hanging them from their saddles or carrying them aloft on spears. Some heads were later nailed to the walls of Celtic dwellings or placed on poles in sanctuaries; others, particularly prized, were embalmed with oil of cedar and kept in coffers as treasures.

Evidence of this head cult has turned up at Roquepertuse and Entremont, both in the south of France, where human skulls taken from the most dangerous enemies, young men in the prime of life, were dramatically and starkly exhibited in stone niches.

A human skull—displayed in a hollow specially designed to hold it—peers out from a limestone pillar, part of the entrance to the Third Century B.C. sanctuary at Roquepertuse in France.

Grim Visages Carved in Stone

Sculptured heads—fashioned by the Celts in all sizes and materials—were often used to supplement real skulls. The so-called *tête coupée*, or severed head, carved and displayed in a sanctuary, was designed to look as if it had actually been cut from a body.

Although there was no standard design or pose, the features generally are broad, with pointed chins, curling ornamental locks and bulging, heavy-lidded eyes. Sometimes, as with the head of a chieftain shown opposite, a torque—the Celtic neck ornament that was endowed with special religious significance—was added beneath the chin, suggesting that the subject possessed divine powers.

Unearthed at Gloucester, England, in 1934, this sad, bulbous-eyed head dates from the First Century A.D. The back of the head is flat, perhaps because it was once fixed to a pillar.

This nine-inch stone effigy of a Celtic warrior's head was discovered in a sanctuary at Entremont, in Provence. Sculpted in the Second Century B.C., it includes a hand, possibly belonging to the victor who severed the head.

The torque-adorned head of an unknown First Century B.C. Celtic chieftain was found in Msecke Zerovice, near Prague, in 1943.

Eight-inch-high twin heads, separated by a bird's curved beak, were unearthed in a Third Century B.C. temple at Roquepertuse.

Multiple Faces for All-seeing Gods

Numerous Celtic divinities were endowed with more than one head, perhaps as a means of intensifying appreciation of their powers.

The three-headed gods may have paralleled the concept of the Christian Trinity: one sacred being with the three different attributes of God as Father, God as Son and God as Holy Spirit. Having three heads also added to a deity's might. Such potency made one of the most malevolent beings of Irish tradition—a three-headed creature named Ellén—even more fearsome. Constant ritual and sacrifice were necessary to prevent her from emerging from her underworld cave and ravaging the land.

Less frequently portrayed are Celtic deities with two faces. Their special power was the ability to look ahead to the next world and, at the same time, to the world of living men.

Among the images of deities on a large terra-cotta vase from Bavay, France, is one figure bearing three heads. Made in the Second Century B.C., the 12-inch-high ceremonial vessel gives visual expression to the Celtic concept of the special threefold nature of divinity.

Masks for Slain Enemies

Metal masks—hollow faces with embossed features—further manifest the strange Celtic head cult. Smaller than life size and fitted with eyeholes once filled with colored glass insets, many of the masks obviously were not designed to be worn by the living; it is possible that they were used as face covers for the dead.

The Roman historian Livy wrote that the Celts decorated severed heads with silver and gold. Since it would have been difficult to gild an actual head, some experts feel that Livy may have been referring to metal masks that were fastened to the skulls of enemies slain in battle.

Curly hair and a beard distinguish this 1,700-year-old bronze mask from Norfolk, England. The eyeholes of the six-inch sculpture, found in 1844, were once plugged with colored glass.

Discovered near Chartres, France, this undated bronze face of a Celt is only four inches high.

This bronze visage of a Celtic deity, from the Pyrenees, was designed with a neck socket so that it could be set on a wooden pole.

Countenances to Ward Off Harm

The Celts were hardly a fearful people —a fact shown time and again as they plunged into the fiercest battles without apparent care for life or limb.

But, though they faced death and the afterlife without apprehension, they were, as Julius Caesar noted, "exceedingly given to religious superstition." They surrounded themselves with all sorts of insignia to ward off the random evils of daily life and to invite the protection of kindly spirits. The human head, since it was deemed to be endowed with special magical powers, was applied by Celtic craftsmen to every imaginable household, stable and personal article.

The bronze head of a man, capped with a crested helmet, once adorned the rim of a wooden bucket, used as the cremation urn for the First Century B.C. grave where it was found.

This two-inch-long bronze brooch of the Fifth Century B.C. came from the grave of a woman near Karlsruhe, in Germany.

Thought to be a harness decoration or a clothing ornament, this three-inch silver disk bears nine faces and is more than 2,000 years old.

Chapter Five: Heroes in Defeat

Even to the eyes of battle-toughened Greek and Roman troops, who were as accustomed to barbarity and bloodshed as they were to victory, the sight of a group of Celtic fighting men amassing for war was terrifying. And so, according to one report based on firsthand knowledge, was the sound. The Greek historian Polybius described this martial assault on the senses in his account of a Roman engagement with some 70,000 Celts in the year 225 B.C. at Telamon, about 80 miles north of Rome. "There were innumerable hornblowers and trumpeters, and as the whole army was shouting its war cries at the same time, there was such a tumult of sound that it seemed that not only the trumpets and the soldiers but all the country round had got a voice and caught up the cry. Very terrifying too were the appearance and gestures of the naked warriors in front, all in the prime of life and finely built men, and all in the leading companies richly adorned with gold torques and armlets."

This was not the first time, nor was it the last, that the behavior of the Celtic fighting man struck terror into the hearts of his opponents. An appalling adversary, he possessed all the physical attributes of a fine warrior, and most of the spiritual ones as well: stature, strength, nerve, courage and pride. He fought with grace and a kind of fierce joy, and although his intentions were bloody, he fought with a certain gallantry, foregoing guile for a direct approach that verged on the naïve.

A Celtic warrior in bronze, naked except for a helmet, a torque and a braided belt, kneels to hurl a spear—long since broken off and lost. Discovered near Rome and probably made during the late Third Century B.C., this five-inch-high figurine expresses the ardent bellicosity of the Celts, who by that time had invaded and settled parts of northern Italy.

But as the military saga of the Celts unfolds, the sad fact emerges that the Celtic warrior, through most of his history, tragically lacked the qualities that might have made him a victor. Although he possessed great courage and determination, he had little or no sense of the teamwork essential to the making of an effective army. Neither did he conceive of warfare as an instrument of nationhood; indeed his only allegiance was to his own tribe and his tribal chieftain. Limited in outlook and in tactical ability, the Celtic warrior desperately needed a charismatic and resourceful figure to lead him. When such a leader finally did appear, ironically, it was too late; for his adversary was Julius Caesar, whose military genius and political ambitions were too much for the Celts.

Beyond all these military considerations, it almost seemed as though fate itself was conspiring against the Celts. For often on those rare occasions when things went well on the field of battle, nature itself intervened, and an earthquake, a storm or some other natural disaster befell the Celts to deprive them of the fruits of their victory.

The bravery and ferocity of the Celtic fighting man were never in doubt. The qualities were evident to his non-Celtic neighbors as early as 400 B.C., when the first waves of Celts pressed over the Alps and into the Etruscan lands of northern Italy. From years of easy living the highly civilized Etruscans were ill-prepared to defend their fields and towns from these wild, shouting men. As the Celts stood outside Clusium, a large and important Etruscan city, its luxury-loving inhabitants were so alarmed by the strange men brandishing strange weapons that they actually appealed for help from the Etruscans' hated enemy,

114

Rome. Emissaries did arrive from Rome but they only managed to deflect the Celts' wrath upon their own capital, by killing a Celtic chieftain.

Scarcely 10 years after the Celts first set foot on Italian soil, a horde of Gauls entered the walls of Rome. The details of the event were reported with shame by the Roman historian Livy. Even before the Celts reached the city, the Romans were in panic. "Terrified townships rushed to arms as the avengers went roaring by; men fled from the fields for their lives; and from all the immense host, covering miles of ground with its struggling masses of horse and foot, the cry went up, 'To Rome!' " Then, as the two armies clashed on the outskirts of the city, the Romans displayed, said Livy, no trace of the old Roman manhood. Officers and men alike fled at the first sound of the Celtic war cry, "hardly waiting even to see their strange enemy from the ends of the earth."

The city gates stood open and the astonished Celts poured in. Behaving like typical conquerors, they roamed through the streets in hordes, admiring, destroying, looting and terrifying the Roman people. "Now here, now there," said Livy, "the yells of triumph, women's screams or the crying of children, the roar of flames or the long rumbling crash of falling masonry forced them [the Romans] to turn their unwilling eyes upon some fresh calamity."

The capture of Rome was the Celts' greatest victory, but the triumph was short-lived. After only seven months, they were driven out of the Roman capital partly by lack of food, partly by dysentery contracted during their occupation. In leaving, the vengeful Celts subjected the Romans to one final act of humiliation: they ordered the city to pay a ransom in gold for its liberation, and produced their own set

A life-sized statue of a nude Celtic fighting man—originally a monument on a 10-foot-high burial mound as sketched below—dates from the Fifth Century B.C. and was excavated in 1962 at Hirschlanden, near Stuttgart, Germany. No one can tell just when it toppled down from the barrow, breaking off its feet during the fall; but a covering of earth protected it from any further damage and it has been preserved as the oldest-known sculpted stone figure of the late Hallstatt period.

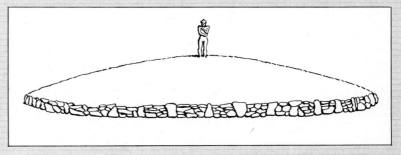

of weights to use in measuring the payment. When the Roman magistrate objected, saying that the Celtic weights were heavier than the ones used by the Romans, the Celtic chieftain insolently flung his own sword on the scale as well, exclaiming, "Woe to the vanquished!"—an expression, said Livy, "intolerable to Roman ears."

Intolerable or not, the Romans did not avenge themselves for the insult until more than 150 years later, in the battle of Telamon whose preparations Polybius described so vividly. Though the sight of Celtic warriors was by that time familiar to the Roman legionaries, their behavior en masse, as Polybius made clear, was still incomprehensible. For example, the nakedness of the Celtic *gaesatae*, or spearmen, was completely misinterpreted. Polybius thought they discarded their clothes for the sake of efficiency. The ground about them, he observed, "was overgrown with brambles which would catch in their clothes and impede the use of their weapons." But Polybius' explanation—plausible as it sounded—was wrong; the custom of disrobing before battle was a ritual—probably with some religious significance—regularly practiced by the *gaesatae*.

Polybius was every bit as astonished by the Celts' fanatical zeal. As Roman javelins fell upon the naked *gaesatae*, he reported that these spearmen, "in their impotent rage, rushed wildly at the enemy and sacrificed their lives." Similarly, when the Roman soldiers penetrated the Celtic host to engage it in hand-to-hand combat, the Celts continued to hold their ground even while being outfought by Roman swordsmen. The Celtic sword, Polybius reported, was inferior, being blunt at the end and good only for cutting, not thrusting. Even so, the Celts wielded it so effectively that after initial encounters with the sword, the Roman army strengthened its shields and substituted metal helmets for leather ones.

The suicidal fury of the Celts at Telamon resulted in a terrible slaughter and a great victory for the Romans. The Celtic dead numbered 25,000, and 8,000 were taken prisoner to be paraded through Rome in triumph by the Roman commander. The defeat signaled the end of a war, "which, if we look at the desperation and daring of the combatants," wrote Polybius, "and the numbers who took part and perished in the battles, is second to no war in history."

As warriors, the Celts made a similar impression on the Greeks. The Celts who invaded Greece were part of a mass movement down the Balkan Peninsula from the heartland of Europe. Led by a chieftain named Brennos, one band of these invaders came purely for booty, including the riches believed to be housed in the sanctuary at Delphi. The Greek historian Pausanias reported on Brennos' adventures, and like Polybius he was especially struck by the Celts' fury when the battle was going badly for them. When their shields failed to protect them from a rain of Greek javelins and arrows, they "rushed at their adversaries like wild beasts, full of rage and temperament, with no kind of reasoning at all; they were chopped down with axes and swords but the blind fury never left them while there was breath in their bodies; even with arrows and javelins sticking through them they were carried on by sheer spirit while their life lasted. Some of them even pulled the spears they were hit by out of their wounds and threw them or stabbed with them."

Pausanias also spoke admiringly of the Celts' horsemanship, noting their custom of sending horse-

Drawn from a damaged original, scenes on a 27-inch bronze Celtic scabbard, engraved in the Fourth Century B.C., present a panorama of war

men into battle accompanied by two mounted retainers who were also expert riders. While the warriors fought, the retainers stood by on the edge of the action, ready to supply fresh mounts as they were needed. If the warrior were killed or wounded, one retainer would take his place in battle while the other carried the warrior back to camp. Thus the real strength of the Celtic cavalry, said Pausanias, was three times what it appeared to be, and the Celts "in the height of the fighting kept the number of their horsemen complete."

Brennos was an astute commander. The route to Delphi led across the Spercheios River and through Thermopylae, and the Greeks tried to stop him at both places. But when his path was barred, he found another one. The Greeks destroyed a bridge over the river, and Brennos simply took 10,000 of his tallest men downstream to a shallow stretch in the dead of night ("and to start with," said Pausanias, "the Celts are the tallest people in the world"); there they either forded the river on foot, swam across or floated to the other side, "using the oblong shields of their country like rafts."

Nonetheless, Brennos never reached his goal. Just short of Delphi he was stopped by a combination of Greek resistance and natural disasters that Pausanias claimed were acts of the gods. An earthquake, lightning and thunder, and a fierce storm were followed by a night of severe frost and snow, coupled with rockfalls. All these elements filled the Celts with such terror that during the night they imagined enemies where none existed. Springing from their sleep they slashed wildly with their swords, killing and maiming one another.

Brennos himself was gravely injured in the last as-

sault on Delphi, and in despair he committed suicide —by drinking unmixed wine, wrote Pausanias. The rest of his army straggled back across the Greek border into Macedonia, where it linked up with another band of Celts and crossed the Dardanelles into Asia Minor. Eventually some of these Celts fought their way inland to the hill country near Ankara, where they established the small kingdom of Galatia. Others roamed over what is now Turkey as plunderers, until they were decisively beaten in the battle of Pergamum in 230 B.C.

After the defeat at Pergamum, the Celtic tide, which had lapped over so much of the Western world, slowly began to ebb. Bold and self-assured Celtic warriors, once so eager for new conquests and riches, now fought desperately just to hold on to what they had. The Roman Empire, pushing its boundaries inexorably outward, incorporated all northern Italy and the portion of France that lies between the Alps and the Pyrenees. One acquisition, made in 121 B.C., was called simply the Province—known today as Provence—and in 59 B.C. the Province acquired a new and ambitious governor, Julius Caesar. Clever, and enormously talented as a military leader, Caesar was to be the nemesis of the Celts.

Ironically, the Celts were not Caesar's main concern when he came to the Province. He came there to establish a power base from which he could launch a political campaign that would make him the sole ruler of Rome. To do so he had to oust Pompey and Crassus, his two fellow members of the ruling triumvirate —a maneuver he may have hoped to accomplish by making himself a popular military hero. In his *Gallic War* Caesar did not say that he deliberately planned

themes: wrestlers in hand-to-hand combat, soldiers with wheels that symbolize war, infantrymen and cavalrymen—one trampling a fallen foe.

to conquer the whole of Gaul. But of course he did so, gaining for himself the needed acclaim and, in the bargain, a fortune in Celtic slaves. Thus the Celts of Gaul, despite gallant if sporadic attempts to protect their independence, ended up as little more than pawns in Caesar's game.

The Celts contributed largely to their own downfall, for Celtic disunity played into Caesar's hands. As countless Latin students have learned, Caesar began his account of the Gallic War by observing that Gaul was divided into three parts. In fact when he first marched into Gaul in 58 B.C., the country was divided into hundreds of large and small tribal holdings, none of them with fixed borders. Congestion, acquisitiveness and love of adventure—the very things that had driven the Celts outward into new lands—also drove them against one another. This, in turn, made them an inviting target for their enemies, so inviting, in fact, that by 58 B.C. the Celts in Gaul were being shoved around by aggressive outsiders. Germanic tribes from beyond the Rhine were pushing into the Celtic lands, forcing the Celts to seek new homes elsewhere.

Caesar's first campaign in Gaul was provoked by just such a migration. The Helvetii, a Celtic tribe living in Switzerland, saw themselves being surrounded by Germans and decided to leave for a less precarious life in western Gaul. To get there they had to cross Rome's Province, and Caesar wanted no part of a Celtic horde—numbering, by their own count, 368,000—disturbing the peace of his territory. Encumbered by their women, children, slaves and wagonloads of household goods, the Helvetii were easy marks for his Roman legionaries. He dogged them for several months and then, in the early sum-

mer of 58 B.C., dealt them a terrible defeat in the battle of Toulon-sur-Arroux. During the battle he captured their commander, and the remaining 130,000 Helvetii straggled back home, a beaten people.

The news of the Helvetian disaster prompted a number of Celtic tribes immediately to approach Caesar with pledges of friendship. When Caesar headed home to the Province at the end of the summer, he could congratulate himself on having subdued about a fifth of Gaul. With their typically divided and parochial outlook, few Celts probably realized at this point that Caesar was taking over their lands piecemeal. But at least one man apparently did. His name was Dumnorix, a nobleman of the Aedui tribe with ambitions to be king. Dumnorix tried to help the Helvetii during their migration; he tried to rally his people against Caesar; and as the war progressed, he tried to get other Celtic tribes to resist the Romans, but his efforts were in vain.

In the north of Gaul a whole group of Celtic tribes, the Belgae, also saw the danger. Caesar's second campaign in Gaul, in the following year, was undertaken specifically to put down a Belgic conspiracy. The Belgae, living where Belgium now lies, were stubborn, tough fighters who boasted that no invading tribes had ever gained a foothold in their territory and none ever would. But they had never confronted an adversary so resourceful as Caesar. He dug trenches, built forts and constructed movable towers from which to fire heavy missiles. Against such methods the Belgae were helpless. In fact the inhabitants of one *oppidum* were so astonished by the moving towers that they simply opened the gates of the town and surrendered.

Caesar completed his campaign against the Belgae

Tributes to a Tough, Tenacious Foe

Classical sculptors who portrayed the Celts in bronze and marble showed them as vanquished foes. But at the same time, they made clear their respect for the physical prowess of the Celts and for the haughty defiance they showed in the face of death.

The marble statues on these pages are Roman copies of long-lost Greek bronzes that probably once crowned a monument in Pergamum, a Greek city on the west coast of present-day Turkey. The monument was erected around 220 B.C. to commemorate the city's victory over Gallic tribes that had settled in Asia Minor some 50 years earlier. The hard fight that the Gauls put up against the Greek legions is evident from these figures, for they portray no weak or cringing enemies but strongly built barbarian warriors. One Classical writer so admired the Celts' daring in battle that he said they "so scorn death that they do battle unclothed except for a girdle."

Rather than face the humiliation of capture, a strapping Gallic warrior has already slain his wife and now turns his sword upon himself. In a detail of the statue, seen above, the strength in the warrior's face as he takes a final backward glance at his foe speaks eloquently of the fierce courage that characterized the Celtic fighting man.

A mortally wounded Gaul is depicted with brutal but respectful realism in this famous figure in Rome's Capitoline Museum. As he slumps upon his shield and broken trumpet awaiting the end, his expression and his furrowed brow, seen in the detail above, betray the bitter anguish of defeat.

in a single summer. By the fall of 57 B.C. he could claim, and did, that most of the Celtic tribes of Gaul had been made subjects of Rome. But most were subjects under duress, and there were frequent acts of rebellion. The Veneti, for instance, who lived on the coast of what is now Brittany, seized two Roman envoys in 56 B.C. and announced that it was better to die as free Celts than to live as Roman slaves. Many of the Veneti's *oppida* sat on headlands accessible only at low tide. Also, the Veneti were seafarers, which made it difficult for Caesar's land-based army to catch up with them.

Yet in the end Caesar beat them at their own game. He attacked the Venetian oak-hulled sailing ships with a fleet of swift galleys built on the spot. The Roman sailors, armed with a makeshift weapon—a hooked knife lashed to a pole—cut the Venetian halyards, brought their sails and rigging tumbling onto the deck and boarded the helpless vessels to slaughter their panic-stricken crewmen and to set the ships ablaze. After several ships had been demolished in this fashion, the Venetian fleet turned and fled. But their luck had run out: the wind died and the fleet lay becalmed. The Roman galleys, powered by oarsmen, overtook the fleet and completely destroyed it. Caesar dealt harshly with the Veneti for their attempted rebellion, executing all their leaders and selling all the men of the tribe into slavery.

Throughout Gaul, as the Celts at last were aroused to the mortal danger posed by Caesar, resistance became a preoccupation, displacing most of the pleasurable aspects of life. Blacksmith shops concentrated on beating out swords and javelins, shields and helmets—weaponry of a strictly utilitarian character, no longer embellished with elegant ceremonial designs. There was no time for fancy as the Gauls turned their whole attention to war.

In 54 B.C., as the war preparations went forward, Caesar, who was about to undertake an expedition into Britain, became so uneasy about a possible Celtic rebellion that he decided to take its potential leaders with him as hostages. One of those leaders was his old enemy Dumnorix, and Dumnorix refused to go. Convinced that Caesar meant to assassinate him as soon as he got him safely outside Gaul, he fled the Roman camp and headed back for his homeland. Caesar sent a cavalry troop to bring him back, with orders to kill Dumnorix if he refused to come —which he did. As the Romans cut him down, he cried repeatedly, "I am a free man in a free state."

With Dumnorix' death, the spirit of Celtic resistance grew even stronger. Soon a major insurrection rose in the land of the Eburones, in what is today Belgium. Led by a patriot named Ambiorix, the Eburones attacked the local Roman garrison, tricked its leaders with a fabric of lies into leaving the Eburones' territory, and then, practicing a guile equal to Caesar's, ambushed and massacred the Roman column as it filed through a narrow ravine.

Elated by the success of this venture, Ambiorix persuaded two Belgic tribes, the Nervii and Aduatuci, to deal similarly with the legions garrisoned on their land. In preparation for this attack, a combined force of Nervii, Aduatuci and Eburones ringed the garrison near present-day Namur with a rampart nine feet high and a trench 15 feet wide. They also constructed scaling towers and grappling hooks just like those used by the Romans. From these siegeworks they showered the thatched roofs of the Roman encampment with red-hot clay pellets and blazing darts, and managed to start a sizable fire. And though ultimately they were driven off by a relieving army commanded by Caesar himself, nevertheless the myth of Roman invincibility had been deflated.

All over Gaul tribes now began to put aside their old rivalries and to work together in the common cause of ridding themselves of Roman rule. In 53 B.C. Indutiomarus, the leader of the Treveri, put together an army consisting of the Senones, Carnutes, Nervii, Aduatuci and Eburones, along with his own forces, which Caesar considered to be the best in Gaul.

Indutiomarus proposed to lead the six tribes in concert and capture the headquarters of Caesar's favorite general, Labienus, located near the modern French city of Mouzon. However, the wily Labienus secretly moved a contingent of cavalry into his camp. Imagining the Romans to be capable of defensive action only, the Celts ringed the garrison and spent the day lobbing missiles over the wall and shouting abuse at the Romans. Labienus sat tight, and then toward evening, when the Celts were lulled into a false sense of superiority, he suddenly opened the gates of the fort and launched a cavalry attack, routing the Celts and killing Indutiomarus.

One after another, Celtic leaders attempted similar uprisings and came to similar ends as Caesar ruthlessly went about demolishing every attempt at revolt. Acco, the leader of an ill-fated revolt among the Senones and the Carnutes, was flogged and put to death before Roman troops. Ambiorix was trailed by a Roman army assigned exclusively to capture him. It never did, but Ambiorix disappeared with a handful of followers into the Ardennes forest, and was never heard from again.

Finally, in 52 B.C., a man emerged who was not only a worthy adversary for Caesar, but possessed a personality forceful enough to unite the dissident Celts and convince them to stay united. His name was Vercingetorix. Described as handsome and exceedingly tall, he was the son of a former chieftain of the Arverni tribe, whose lands encompassed modern Auvergne. Like any Celtic nobleman of his day, Vercingetorix was headstrong and ambitious, sure of himself and resentful of higher authority. Yet he was also thoughtful and farsighted: he did not leap into situations without studying them first, and he planned his moves in advance, making whatever preparations were needed to carry them through successfully. In addition, he was shrewdly cognizant of human nature: he knew when to use flattery, when to use force, and how to make people rise above petty rivalries and work in unison for the Celtic cause.

In the winter of 53-52 B.C. a group of Celtic chieftains met to plan a joint action against Caesar, vowing to fight to the death, because, as Caesar himself later said, they thought it better "to be slain in battle than to fail to recover their old renown in war and the liberty they had received from their forefathers."

Caesar does not say whether Vercingetorix was present at this war council, but he probably was, for he immediately urged the Arverni to join the rebellion. When the tribal elders held back, he raised a ragtag army of his own, used it to seize control of his tribe and rallied the Arverni people to his support. In short order he became commander of all the rebels.

Vercingetorix immediately sent delegates through all of central and western Gaul to requisition men and arms for a supreme effort against Caesar. By using peruasion, bribes and threats he amassed a fighting force that represented three quarters of Gaul, and was virtually a national army. But it was never a true army. Instead of being organized into divisions, it fought as a coalition of tribal units, each unit commanded by its own tribal chieftain. Given the personal ambitions of the individual leaders and the none-too-friendly relations of some of the tribes, it was not an easy army to control. Yet Vercingetorix succeeded in holding it together by a combination of tact and discipline. He met with his chieftains daily to discuss objectives and assign missions, and he dealt severely with waverers, sending them home, Caesar said, with their ears cut off and one eye gouged out "to point a moral to the rest."

From his tactics it seems evident that Vercingetorix had studied the Roman military system and detected its weaknesses. In recruiting warriors, for instance, he asked especially for horsemen, knowing they would be essential in the hit-and-run war he meant to wage against the Romans. He had also noticed that the Roman troops fought best when Caesar was present, and in one of his very first actions he tried —unsuccessfully, as it turned out—to prevent Caesar from joining his legions.

Caesar's dependence upon forage for his army was another weakness, and Vercingetorix exploited it by using his cavalry to intercept Caesar's foraging parties. He also instituted a policy of burning stores of grain to prevent Caesar's getting them. In fact, it was this policy that precipitated Vercingetorix' first major engagement with the Romans.

The engagement took place at Avaricum, near the modern city of Bourges, in the land of the Bituriges, through which a Roman army was passing. Vercingetorix sent messengers to the Bituriges, urging them

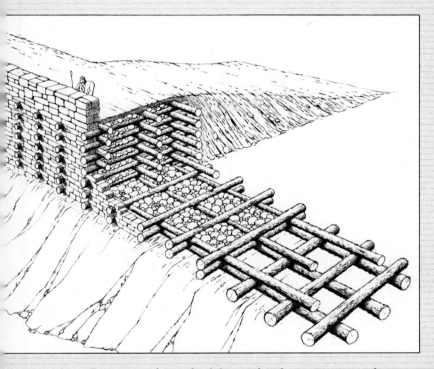

Resistant to fire and solid enough to be secure against battering rams, the Gallic wall, or murus gallicus—so named by Julius Caesar, who encountered it during his campaigns against the Gauls—was a design used for Celtic strongholds. The diagram above reveals the sturdy construction. The core was a criblike framework of timbers laid lengthwise and crosswise and lashed or nailed together, where they intersected, for maximum strength: the spaces between were filled with stones and rubble. Stone masonry formed a fireproof facing for the outside wall. Earthen ramps were butted against the inner face of the wall, giving the defending Celts easy access to their battle stations behind the protective stone parapet.

to burn their towns so that Caesar would be deprived of supplies. The reluctant Bituriges finally agreed but they begged Vercingetorix to allow them to spare one —Avaricum, their principal town and the ornament of their culture. Finally, against his better judgment, Vercingetorix acquiesced and stood by with a force of warriors to help in the defense of the *oppidum*.

Despite Avaricum's strategic position (*pages 124-125*), Caesar was set on taking it: Avaricum was a grain depot, and his army's food supplies—thanks to the new Celtic tactics—were running dangerously low. In his usual methodical fashion Caesar encamped at the only convenient approach to the town and began to build massive scaling towers and two broad ramps leading to Avaricum's walls. Meanwhile the Celts, who had learned a thing or two about defensive techniques in the years they had been the victims of Roman siege tactics, resisted the Romans fiercely. They lassoed Roman grappling hooks and dragged them inside the walls with windlasses. They tunneled under the Roman ramp, using techniques they had developed as iron miners, and set fire to its wooden supports. As the Roman siege towers rose, Vercingetorix had towers built on Avaricum's walls just as high or higher and covered them—as Caesar covered parts of his siegeworks—with hides as protection against burning missiles. When the Roman troops moved their towers against Avaricum's, the defenders met them with volleys of stones, hot pitch and boiling fat.

But Avaricum's determined defenders were no match for the persistent Romans. As the assault continued, Vercingetorix saw that the fate of Avaricum was sealed and tried to withdraw his troops. They were prevented from leaving, ironically, by the wom-

Siegeworks at a Doomed Town

One of the bitterest clashes in the Celts' history was their 27-day defense of the Gallic town of Avaricum. In order to capture it and the large supply of grain so essential to the starving Roman army, Caesar ordered that the colossal siegeworks diagramed on these pages be erected before the wall guarding the town. With timber felled in nearby forests, the Romans built assault towers 80 feet high —ramps nearly 400 feet long over which the towers could be rolled—and an 80-foot-high terrace for artillery pieces. What few cattle Caesar could round up were slaughtered, and their fresh hides used as flame-resistant coverings for the wooden sheds under which Roman soldiers moved construction materials and artillery. But the Gauls retaliated in kind, raising countertowers on the wall, boring a tunnel into one of the Roman ramps and starting a fire in a futile attempt to demolish the entire structure.

By the 25th day of the siege, the Roman works (blue) were ready for use in the storming of Avaricum (tan). Roman assault towers (A) on the earth-and-timber ramps (B) loomed above the Gallic wall (C). Roman legionaries under the artillery gallery (D) maintained a deadly barrage of javelins and steel arrows fired from mounted crossbows, while soldiers at long range (E) manned catapults to launch a hail of heavy missiles. The Gauls, in the meanwhile, had raised their countertowers (F) and completed the tunnel (G) into the Roman ramp. Early on the 26th day, the Romans saw the ramp smoldering and withdrew one of their towers. Protected by the covered sheds (H), they ran to smother the fire. On the 27th day the Romans destroyed one Gallic tower and swarmed over a drawbridge (I) onto the Gallic wall. A hideous massacre ensued and only a ragtag band of Celts (J) managed to escape.

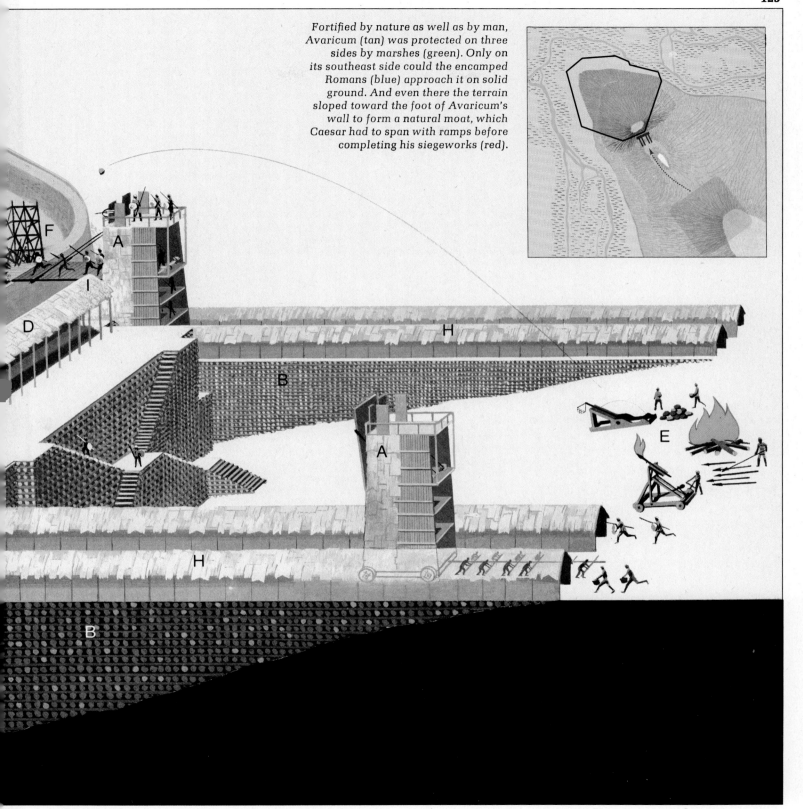

Fortified by nature as well as by man, Avaricum (tan) was protected on three sides by marshes (green). Only on its southeast side could the encamped Romans (blue) approach it on solid ground. And even there the terrain sloped toward the foot of Avaricum's wall to form a natural moat, which Caesar had to span with ramps before completing his siegeworks (red).

en of Avaricum, who set up howls of protest alerting the Romans to the planned escape. Then fresh disasters befell the Celts. It began to rain heavily, and the men who were manning the town wall took shelter, foolishly leaving their defense works unattended. Seizing the opportunity, Caesar's troops poured over the wall and through Avaricum's streets, killing its citizens right and left. According to Caesar, no one was spared, neither "old men, nor women, nor children." Of Avaricum's 40,000 inhabitants, only 800 managed to escape and, led by Vercingetorix, made their way to safety.

But Vercingetorix was not discouraged by this disaster. Immediately he called together his chieftains, and using his gifts as an orator persuaded them not to abandon the cause. He reminded them that the defense of Avaricum had never been a wise course, and he promised that he would rally support for the revolt from tribes that were not yet part of the confederation. Making good on his promise, he sent emissaries throughout Gaul to recruit fresh troops, asking them especially to seek out archers. Never before used against Caesar, these Celtic archers quite suddenly improved both the morale and the effectiveness of Vercingetorix' army.

For several days Caesar rested his troops at Avaricum and replenished his badly depleted supplies. Then he set out in pursuit of Vercingetorix, who by this time had reached Gergovia, the chief town of his own Arverni people and the center of the Celtic rebellion. Gergovia sat atop a mountain and was practically impregnable. Caesar tried by various means to lure Vercingetorix down into the valley, but Vercingetorix wisely refused to be enticed into a fixed battle on level ground where the experienced Roman legions could outmaneuver him. Instead he harassed the Romans almost daily with lightning cavalry raids, placing his archers among the horsemen to increase their striking power.

Caesar finally tried to take Gergovia by assault, feinting an attack from one direction while actually approaching from another. But just as the first wave of Roman soldiers reached the walls of the mountaintop *oppidum,* they were set upon by Celts from an unexpected quarter and were forced to retreat. Indeed, the retreat was apparently a rout, for Caesar himself admitted that at the end of the engagement 700 men were missing.

The news of this Roman fiasco traveled throughout Gaul, and soon the countryside resounded to the marching feet of new recruits for Vercingetorix' army. After seven years of war, it seemed that all Gaul was finally united. The Celtic army was swelled by tens of thousands of men, many of them from tribes that had at one time been Rome's allies. Marching day and night through the territories of whatever remaining friends he could find, Caesar headed south, with the Celtic army close on his heels.

In the summer of 52 B.C. Vercingetorix set up headquarters at the fortified town of Alesia, near modern Dijon, and from there sent a force to cut off the Roman legionaries from their supply train. The ambush failed and Caesar's army turned in its tracks. Trailing the Celts back to Alesia, Caesar laid siege to the town—setting in motion what was to be the war's climactic engagement.

Vercingetorix had previously stockpiled Alesia with enough provisions to last a garrison of 20,000 men through 30 days. Probably he thought he could safely hold out against a blockade until help arrived, but this was a miscalculation. So, too, was his decision to send out his entire cavalry to recruit aid for the embattled fortress, leaving himself without a mobile force to forage for additional food and with no means of interfering with Caesar's siege operations. Thus Caesar was free to construct some of the most elaborate military works of his entire career. The Roman fortifications at Alesia included a ring of two parallel trenches 20 feet wide into which water was deflected from neighboring streams to form a moat; a rampart and palisades 12 feet high with turrets set at 80-foot intervals; fields of what Caesar called *stimuli,* iron barbs driven into the ground and lightly covered over; and eight rows of pits covered by brush, with sharp stakes set into the pit bottom to form a hideous kind of mantrap.

Within Alesia, the Celts observed these preparations with mounting apprehension and sinking morale. As days wore into weeks and food supplies grew low, there was talk of resorting to cannibalism, using for this, Caesar reported, "the bodies of those whose age had shown them useless for war." Finally, after almost a month, help did arrive: a huge force that Caesar estimated as a quarter of a million men stretching for three miles along the Alesian plain.

At the sight of these reinforcements, the Celts' spirits rose, but the two armies had difficulty communicating across the Roman works that ringed the *oppidum.* Watching from Alesia's walls, Vercingetorix tried with little success to coordinate his activities with those of the relieving army. As the new recruits attacked the Roman position with slings, arrows and stones from the outside, Vercingetorix led a force out of the town to throw hurdles across the Roman trench nearest the town, and fill it with dirt. But the Romans had dug in too securely. The Celts were "caught unawares on the *stimuli,* or they sank in the pits and were impaled, or they were shot by heavy javelins from the ramparts and the turrets, and so perished on every side." After four days of such futile efforts, the relieving army simply gave up and melted away.

His position now impossible, Vercingetorix called together his chieftains on the following morning and said that as he had undertaken his campaign for the liberty of his people rather than any personal gain, he was now prepared to offer himself as hostage to the Romans in whatever form the Romans wanted him, dead or alive. They surrendered him alive, and Caesar ordered him taken back to Rome, where in 45 B.C. he was paraded as a captive through the streets. Immediately afterward he was executed as a dangerous enemy of the Roman people.

With the death of Vercingetorix, Gaul was finished; oblations to the gods, Druidic sacrifices, Celtic oratory and Celtic valor—all were unavailing. Though resistance smoldered and flickered for another year, never again were the Celts any real threat to Rome. After Caesar, the Roman general Claudius crossed the English Channel to complete what Caesar had begun, the conquest of Britain. Most of the Celtic world lay prostrate, its fields wasted, its language obliterated, its gods disguised as Roman gods.

Only in Ireland did the old ways live on. Locked behind its coastline, denied the advantages of Roman roads and aqueducts that now threaded southern Britain, but preserved from the ruinous effects of conflict with Rome, Ireland remained a world unto itself. It was in this world, more than anywhere else, that the ancient Celtic legends and laws, the Celtic symbols and the Celtic voice were kept alive.

Of all the paradoxes in the story of the Celts, none is stranger than the form in which their culture survived after their conquest by Rome. From the days glorified in blood-spilling legend as the Age of Heroes there emerged a new Celtic era known—of all things—as the Age of Saints. Operating under the aegis of a branch of the Christian Church that was established in Ireland, Celtic scholars enriched the intellectual life of Europe. They founded monasteries, served as teachers to the members of royal courts and created a literature distinguished by its style, scholarship, imagery and wit.

Out of the nonliterate learning of the bards and Druids there blossomed a new literary heritage —which along with the Celts' artistic achievement constitutes their great gift to the modern world. Unlike their material achievements, many of which could not withstand the ravages of time, the Irish Celts' intellectual gift was indestructible. More than half a millennium after this legacy was formed, it inspired and shaped some of the loveliest poetry and prose of modern times. And, ironically, this heritage from the fatally disunited Celts became the moving spirit of one of the world's most staunchly nationalistic people: the Irish.

Phoenix-like, this literary legacy took shape during a period when most of the once-great Celtic world lay in ruins. By the end of the First Century A.D. Roman victories in Gaul and Britain had replaced the

Familiar Celtic motifs—whorls, crosshatches and stern, almond-eyed faces—embellish the Christ and other figures on this Seventh Century A.D. representation of the Crucifixion from Ireland. Wrought of gilt bronze, the piece is eight inches high and has holes at the corners, indicating that it once served as an ornamental plate for the front cover of a book.

Celtic tribal suzerainties with Roman bureaucracy. The old Celtic gods of the Druids had merged with the gods of Rome. Celtic *oppida* had become Romanized market towns; Celtic craftsmen, though their skill was undiminished, now produced wares of Roman design; and Celtic noblemen lived in villas identical to the fine houses of gentlemen in Rome, with elaborate mosaic floors of Classical design, heated by warm air from underground furnaces. Young Celtic men served in the Roman army. Many went off to man a new complex of Roman border forts in Gaul, intended to hold off the latest wave of invasions from the north: tribesmen whom the Romans labeled variously as Teutones and Germani.

Even in Britain, where the Roman presence was far less pervasive, little was left of the old Celtic way of life. When the Romans pulled out of Britain in 367 A.D., having found it impossible to govern the Britons without a constant show of force, their place was quickly taken by other invaders, the Angles and the Saxons, and the island's Celtic inhabitants were once again submerged in another culture. In the wake of these invasions, Britain's Celtic peoples survived only in Wales, in Scotland and on the Isle of Man. One group emigrated back to the ancestral homeland on the European Continent and established a new kingdom in the old Celtic land of Armorica, in the region now called Brittany.

Across the Irish Sea from Britain, however, life went on as before. Invaded by neither Romans nor Angles nor Saxons, the people of Ireland remained intransigently Celtic. They preserved their Celtic inheritance with a tenacity that extended even to the invention of a mythological origin that made the Irish Celts a chosen people. Concocted no one knows when, but set down in writing by Irish scribes sometime in the Middle Ages, this extraordinary pseudohistory, which is called the *Book of Invasions,* purports to prove that the Irish people are a race descended from the gods.

According to the *Invasion* tales, Ireland was settled by a succession of diverse peoples, the last of whom were the Celts—in the tales called the Milesians or Sons of Mil. Bearing such names as the Cessair, the Parthelonians, the Nemedians, the Fir Bolg, the Fomoiri and the Tuatha De Danaan, these mythical Irish ancestors were said to possess some remarkable characteristics. The Cessair, for instance, were a breed whose women outnumbered the men by a ratio of three to one, while the Fomoiri were bizarre warlike creatures each with one eye, one arm, one leg and two ominous sets of teeth.

The pious monks, who lovingly set down great numbers of traditional Irish tales, did not always vouch for the accuracy of their contents. "I do not accept as a matter of certain belief certain things in this history," cautioned one unidentified scribe. "Some things are diabolic impositions, some are poetic inventions, some have a semblance of truth, some have not, and some are meant for entertaining fools." Yet there are elements in many of the ancient tales that are not pure fiction. The famous Ulster Cycle, which contains the tale *The Cattle Raid of Cooley,* describes an Ireland divided into four kingdoms: Connaught, where Queen Medb is sovereign; Ulster, where King Conchobar rules; and two other kingdoms, Leinster and Munster. The four kingdoms are, of course, the four main provinces of Ireland.

The Ireland of the legendary tales was a country known as Eriu, and its dominant people were the Goi-

dels, a name attached to them by Celts living in Wales. (Actually the Welsh name was Gwyddel, but the Irish Celts pronounced it as Goidel, later as Gaodhel and finally, in modern Irish, as Gael.) The Goidels spoke a different form of Celtic from their British cousins. Because of this difference in language, the origin of the Irish Celts remains a mystery. Some say the Goidels came to Ireland directly from the Continent; others contend that they were emigrants from an early Celtic occupation of Britain. In any case by the Fifth Century A.D.—when legends give way to history—the Goidels were well established all through the land by then called Ireland.

In the north of Ireland, by 400 A.D., the people were ruled by a strong dynastic Goidel family known as the Ui Neill. The founder of the dynasty was a Celtic prince, Niall of the Nine Hostages, who ruled his kingdom from an ancient royal center called Tara, and Niall and his many sons subsequently took over most of the central part of the country as well. Niall's eldest son, Loegaire, said to be the first king of Tara, was crowned either in 427 or 428 A.D. The power of the Ui Neill in the north was matched in the south by a confederation of Munster princes calling themselves the Eóganachta. Northern Ireland was thereafter known as Leth Cuinn, or Conn's Half, southern Ireland as Leth Moga Nuatha, or Mug's Half, after two mythical Irish ancestors of the peoples of the Ui Neill and the Eóganachta.

During this earliest period of Irish history, the raiding and skirmishing so typical of ancient Celtic life continued unabated. The Ui Neill and the Eóganachta constantly violated each other's borders, and they were directly or indirectly responsible for the establishment of several Goidelic kingdoms across the

The Saint Who Christianized a Pagan Land

On a 15th Century grave marker from a churchyard in County Louth, Ireland, St. Patrick appears in bishop's garb, looming above a snake—the creature with which his name is always linked in folklore. But neither the familiar legend, nor the serene likeness of the saint on the 52-inch stone carving, conveys the intense spirit of the man who brought Christianity to the Celts in the last stronghold of their culture.

According to his own writings—the only contemporary account of his life—Patrick was born on the west coast of Britain about 385 A.D., the son of Calpornius, a Roman official. Raised on the estate of his father, who was a Christian, the boy was captured by Irish pirates when he was 16, brought to Ireland and sold into slavery.

In captivity the once-privileged and carefree youth was set to tending sheep in the service of a wealthy farmer. Overwhelmed by loneliness and humiliation, he found strength in prayer and experienced a profound religious awakening. Later, looking back on his youth, he saw divine justice in his early suffering and wrote in his *Confession,* "I did not know the true God. I was taken into captivity with many thousands of people, because we turned away from God and did not keep His commandments."

After six years of servitude, Patrick

heeded an inner voice telling him to set out for a ship at a distant harbor that would carry him to freedom. When he arrived at the port, the heathen captain and his crew first refused to take him aboard, but finally relented after he had prayed to God. Three days later, he landed on what was probably the coast of Gaul.

Patrick's account of his life leaves the next 20 years largely unexplained. He is believed to have studied under Germanus of Auxerre, Gaul's most eminent priest. Germanus is credited by some scholars with having secured Patrick's appointment as Bishop of Ireland. But according to the saint himself, the call came from the Lord in a dream in which the Irish people cried out: "We ask thee, boy, come and walk among us once more."

Patrick spent the last 30 years of his life in Ireland. The famous legend that he drove the snakes out of the land is apocryphal, but his real accomplishments were formidable. Despite the opposition of the Druids, he won countless converts to Christianity and promoted the founding of many churches and monasteries. Just before his death in 462 A.D., he mounted one of the highest peaks in Ireland and blessed the country's assembled tribes. Today that peak is known as Croagh Patrick, and Patrick himself is still Ireland's patron saint.

One of the oldest treasures now surviving from the Celtic Christian monasteries is the Seventh Century A.D. Book of Durrow, a nine-by-five-inch manuscript containing the four Gospels and a series of highly decorative, imaginative paintings. The pattern of intricate, abstract designs at the right, painted on vellum around 650 A.D., is called a carpet page for its resemblance to the opulent carpets of Persia.

Irish Sea. The Ui Neill, for instance, were traditionally credited with forcing one small pocket of older Celtic peoples to flee their homeland in the north of Ireland for Scotland. There they settled a stretch of the Argyll coast and established the Scottish kingdom of Dál Riata. In the south raiding parties of Eóganachta descended on Wales, intermarried with dynastic British families and created Welsh Goidelic kingdoms. (From one such alliance may have come the romantic legend of the Welsh knight Tristram, who was sent to escort the Irish princess Isolde to her marriage with the Welsh king Mark of Cornwall.)

In the midst of this intermittent strife and tumult, another gentler conquest was taking place as the Christian religion entered Ireland. How it got there is somewhat obscure. Perhaps it came by way of Britain, where bishops from Rome were active as early as the Fourth Century A.D. Perhaps it arrived from Brittany, brought by missionaries from Roman Gaul. According to the ancient records of the Catholic Church, Pope Celestine sent a bishop named Palladius to Ireland on an apostolic mission in 431 A.D., an assignment that suggests the existence of a Christian community large enough to justify the trip. St. Patrick (page 131), however, is the man traditionally credited with—and still revered for—bringing Christianity to Irish soil.

Although St. Patrick did not singlehandedly convert all Ireland, the extent of his influence there, in what he himself called "the ends of the earth," is undeniable. The seat of his church was at Armagh in the territory of the Ui Neill, and its administration was thoroughly Roman, which meant that it was organized and run by an ecclesiastical hierarchy according to the canons formulated by the mother church in Rome. But in spite of the official character of Patrick's church, Christianity in Ireland took on a distinctively Celtic cast: abbots in the Irish monasteries, although adhering to Roman creed, preferred to operate as independent self-governing enclaves. In a spirit rooted in old Celtic tribal ways, Ireland's early monasteries ran their own shows.

By the Sixth Century A.D. these Irish monastic communities were as well known for learning as for their asceticism. Men came to them both to be educated, and to worship God in a kind of isolation offered by few other monastic establishments. With the blessings of their abbots, Irish monks were permitted to go off and live as hermits in the most remote places they could find. In the Scottish Hebrides and on bleak islands off Irish shores their shelters—sturdy little structures of stone, shaped like beehives (pages 146-147)—can still be seen.

To one of these isolated islands off the Scottish coast—Iona—came the monk whose zeal spread the Irish idea of monasticism throughout Britain. His name was St. Colum Cille—he is also often called St. Columba—and like most of the saints in the Age of Saints he achieved sanctity by his good works rather than by any act of martyrdom. Colum Cille was born a prince of the Ui Neill, but he renounced his rank and his family name to devote his life to the service of God. For all his spirituality, however, Colum Cille was also a man of action. He organized a monastery on Iona and from this base he set out to Christianize the Picts on the mainland of Scotland. Monasteries modeled on the original one at Iona sprang up throughout the Scottish Kingdoms and from there spread into what is now England and Wales.

The students who entered Colum Cille's monasteries came partly for religious teaching but also because the monasteries had a reputation for general scholarship. They were in effect educational institutions, and the schooling was of course cost-free, or nearly so. There was no tuition, the books were supplied and few of the monasteries required payment for room and board beyond some sort of work in the monastic community—such as fishing, tending crops, copying manuscript books or building.

Many of the monks were probably former bards, and with their lifelong training in the Druidic tradition of spoken literature, they must have had little trouble mastering Latin and memorizing the chants and responses of the Christian liturgy. Some, in fact, borrowed the Roman alphabet to create a written form of Goidelic and used it to transcribe their own Irish legends, genealogies and laws into one of the earliest Western vernacular literatures.

In the austerity and solitude of Iona and its offspring monasteries, recluse scribes and artisans also created a typically Celtic Christian art that was the very antithesis of their stark physical surroundings. Drawing upon the traditional art of their pagan past, Irish monks decorated their sacred manuscript books and the accouterments of their churches with designs that are a breathtaking reminder of the La Tène art of their forebears.

Reliquaries, crosiers and chalices are fashioned with intricately interwoven strands of gold filigree inset with brilliant multicolored nuggets of enamel and glass (pages 142-143). In the sacred books—some produced in St. Colum Cille's own monastery—margins overflow with patterns of swirling, interlocking lines, and entire pages are given over to scriptural pic-

Gaily clad, a man—the symbol of St. Matthew—stares stonily from the frontispiece page to the Gospel of St. Matthew in the Book of Durrow. The patterns on his lavish checkerboard cloak foreshadow the delicate enamelwork done by Irish craftsmen (pages 142-143). While the figure faces forward, the feet are seen in profile—a stylistic quirk that the Celtic monks adopted from the work of Christian artists in Egypt.

tures that are a kaleidoscope of color and restless patterns. In one, a man—the symbol of a saint—stands gaudily clad in a checkerboard cloak framed by a vinelike interlace of multishaded strands at left. Perhaps the most famous of these Bible pages are the dazzling "carpet pages" (pages 133, 136, 139), covered in their entirety with patterns that rival the delicacy of the finest metalwork and the brilliance of enamel or precious stones.

The loosely affiliated network of monasteries unofficially called the Celtic Church, where this magnificent art flourished, dominated Christianity in the British Isles for almost 400 years. But, alas, the monasteries themselves were doomed. Sometime after St. Colum Cille's death in 597, Viking raiders from Scandinavia began to descend on the island of Iona. Within 200 years all the resident monks had been massacred. On the Irish mainland the monasteries were also the object of Viking aggression. And there another disruptive force contributed to the monasteries' downfall. Young men of noble birth were entering the Church just as Colum Cille had done, but unlike him, they were not satisfied with the austere monastic environment; they preferred to surround themselves with the luxurious worldly goods that had been anathema to the monks of earlier generations. Deeply dismayed by this corrupting spirit, great numbers of the older, more serious monks sadly began to leave their retreats to become wanderers —or peregrini. Others left to be missionaries who would carry the faith abroad.

Many of the peregrini voyaged to the Continent, where the Irish reputation for scholarship had preceded them, largely through the influence of a prior Irish wanderer named St. Columbanus. Several cen-

turies before, around the year 590, Columbanus had left Ireland and had found a ready welcome in several European courts. He settled in Burgundy long enough to establish three monastic retreats. But although St. Columbanus was admired for his scholarship, the worldly Burgundian court soon grew tired of his strict moral views. He was threatened with execution for refusing to baptize a nobleman's illegitimate child, but his life was eventually spared on the condition that he leave Burgundy.

With his faithful friend St. Gall, another Irish expatriate, Columbanus moved on to Switzerland, where Gall left him to found the famous monastery bearing his name, St. Gall. Columbanus himself continued across the Alps into Lombardy, where he built the equally famous monastery of Bobbio. Both St. Gall and Bobbio became important scholastic centers, attracting some of the finest minds of the day. Bobbio, for instance, contained a remarkable library of some 700 manuscripts. Although some were original creations, most were copies of books borrowed from other libraries in a regular system of exchange, rather like a modern interlibrary loan arrangement.

The library at Bobbio was largely devoted to sacred works, but not exclusively so. It also contained dictionaries, glossaries, and texts on such subjects as music, grammar and mathematics. It even included "profane"—that is, secular—works by Classical authors such as Virgil, Horace, Juvenal, Ovid, Cicero, Seneca and Pliny the Elder.

The majority of Bobbio's books were probably produced in its own scriptorium, or writing studio, and many of the scribes who wrote them were originally Irish. On some of their manuscripts they penned marginal notes in Goidelic in a distinctive Irish script

The Lindisfarne Gospel, named for the Northumbrian monastery where it was produced in the late Seventh Century A.D., is embellished with five intricate paintings known as carpet pages, including the spectacular one at left. In and around the arms of the Christian cross, restless barbarian designs—most conspicuously the omnipresent whorls favored by the early Celtic artisans—fill every cranny of space.

style known as half uncial. Their marginal jottings enliven the manuscripts with comments on the coldness of the weather or the hairiness of the vellum, which made good penmanship difficult. Probably these asides were the monks' way of circumventing the scriptorium's strict rule of silence.

At St. Gall, too, the scholarly tradition of the early Celtic monks flourished; there the emphasis was on education. St. Gall had two schools, one for students who had taken religious vows, the other for the laity; they were called respectively the *schola claustri* and the *schola exterior*. In both schools young boys were taught to read and write Latin, to memorize the Book of Psalms and to know enough about music to take part in church services. There were also lessons in the trivium: grammar, rhetoric and logic. Beyond this elementary schooling there were advanced studies in the quadrivium: arithmetic, geometry, astronomy and music. Discipline in the older grades was especially severe; the pupils were forbidden to speak anything but Latin, for instance, and the penalty for disobeying the rule was flogging.

In the several centuries that followed their founding, both St. Gall and Bobbio became rallying points for the stream of Irish *peregrini* that began to pour through Europe with the decline of the Irish monasteries. Indeed one writer of the period observed that wandering seemed to have become second nature to the Irish. Two of the *peregrini* found their way to the court of Charlemagne, and the Emperor established monastic schools for them, one in the northern part of his empire at Liège, a second at Pavia in Italy. For a third Celtic monk, named Dicuil, Charlemagne supplied lodgings within one of his palaces and made him a teacher-in-residence.

Dicuil is noted for a number of scholarly contributions. He wrote a geography that is interesting chiefly for its mention of Iceland, which he said had been seen by Ireland's hermit-monks, and also for its description of an elephant presented as a gift to Charlemagne by the Caliph of Bagdad. Dicuil was also an astronomer, and in this capacity he worked out mathematical rules for determining the age of the moon, the date of Easter and the length of the lunar and solar years. And long before most men even entertained such ideas, Dicuil speculated on ways of computing the distances between the earth and the planets, and the planets' revolutions.

Another Irish monk who took refuge at the Carolingian court and received a cordial welcome was Sedulius Scottus. Around 848 Sedulius journeyed to Liège—capital city of Charlemagne's grandson Charles the Bold—and immediately dazzled everyone with his wit and erudition. He knew Latin supremely well and wrote delightful verse, much of it in praise of his princely patrons. Urbane, fond of conversation, good food and fine wine, Sedulius once scribbled a playful petition to the Bishop of Liège in the form of a poem, pleading with the bishop for better quarters and asking him to improve the quality of the monastery table with such fare as honey, meat and wine.

Among Sedulius' circle of friends in the Liège monastery was another Irish scholar with a similar name, Johannes Scottus Eriugena, who had a similar talent for Latin and also for Greek. But where Sedulius was brilliant, Johannes was profound. In fact Johannes may have influenced the course of the humanism of the Middle Ages even more than Columbanus. Johannes' views of God and the world were incorporated into a scholarly treatise, *De divisione naturae*, which has been called the first great philosophical work of Western Europe. A blend of rationalism and mysticism, of neoplatonic ideas and Christian theology, *De divisione naturae* hints at concepts that were explored in much greater depth by the great Thomas Aquinas 400 years later.

Though deep in piety and elevated in scholarship, the Irish monks also enjoyed writing about less taxing matters. Like countless Celtic bards before them, they delighted in spinning tales, called *immrama*, about heroes and their adventures—although now, to be sure, the heroes were Christians. One of the most famous *immramas* tells of St. Brendan, a monk who went on a fantastic voyage. In real life Brendan was the founder of the monastery of Clonfert in County Galway in the Sixth Century. In the tale, *Navigatio Brendani*, he decides to set off for the Land of Promise of the Saints, which he has seen in a vision. With 14 other monks he sails westward toward many adventures. He meets Judas Iscariot sitting on a rock resting from his exertions in hell; on Easter eve Brendan lands on an island to celebrate the Resurrection and discovers that the island is the back of a whale. He savors many marvelous foods that appear fresh daily, and encounters a spring whose waters put men to sleep. Finally he reaches the Land of Promise of the Saints and then returns to Ireland to tell the people about it.

So popular was Brendan's tale that it circulated throughout Western Christendom. Irish *peregrini* translated it into the vernacular languages of whatever land they lived in, and versions of it have been found in Norman-French, Old French, Middle English, Flemish, Dutch, German, Provençal, Italian and Norse—as well as, of course, the original Irish. In fact the tale of Brendan's voyages westward to the Land of Promise was so vivid in the minds of its hearers that, as late as the 18th Century, map makers included it on their charts of the Atlantic Ocean. Some believers thought the imagined island was real and that it might have served as a way station for sailors' journeys to the New World—or even that it was the New World itself. Hence Brendan's voyages were sometimes cited as evidence that the Irish were the first to set foot on the North American continent.

Besides composing tales of saintly adventures that were thinly veiled versions of the old pagan epics, the Irish monks sometimes allowed their contemplations to stray entirely from spiritual matters. The monks' worldly thoughts, too, often found expression in poetry, much of which has been translated by 19th Century Irish and English scholars, who painstakingly preserved the spirit—and often the rhyme—of the original stanzas.

One unknown monk stole time from his studies to celebrate the signs of oncoming winter in a poem whose brisk images and rhythms foretell the season:

News I bring:/bells the stag,
winter snow,/summer past;
wind high and cold,/low the sun,
short its courts,/seas are strong;
russet bracken,/shape awry,.
wild goose raises/wonted cry;
cold lays hold/on wings of bird
icy time:/this I heard.

Another monk with a wandering mind looked up from his spiritual tasks, and let himself be enticed into basking in the beauties of nature:

A wall of forest looms above,
and sweetly the blackbird sings;
all the birds make melody
over me and my books and things.

There sings to me the cuckoo
from bush-citadel in gray hood.
God's doom! May the Lord protect me,
writing well, under the great wood.

But for a third monk the distractions of the world were of another kind, and perhaps he tried to exorcise them by penning a poetic confession:

A shame on my thinking,
how it wanders away;
it will cause me embarrassment
on Last Judgment Day.

At psalm-time it rushes forth
on a pathway that's odd,
running, raving, misbehaving
in the presence of God.

To merry women's company,
the unvirtuous kind,
through wood and through cities
faster than the wind.

At the conclusion of this poem, some nine stanzas later, the poet adds a final penitential verse, hoping that he may "come to Christ at last," for "He is no unsteady thing, not wandering like me."

Today the surviving manuscripts of these pensive poems and magical tales, along with the Irish monks' loving transcriptions of the epic adventures of their ancestors, are the treasured possessions of museums and libraries in several European cities. Some of them, appropriately enough, are in the archives of the Royal Irish Academy in Dublin, and it was from this national treasure that modern Irishmen drew sustenance for the movement that came to be known as the Irish literary revival.

Immersing themselves in the tales and poems, borrowing the heroic themes and lyrical style of their long-dead literary predecessors, writers like William Butler Yeats, John Millington Synge and Lady Gregory in effect resurrected the Celtic past.

The pivotal figure of this literary revival was Yeats, whose gifts and ideas first inspired a loosely affiliated group of artists and intellectuals with aims and objectives that ranged—in a fashion reminiscent of the Celts of old—from the sublimely esthetic to the mundanely political.

But the catalyst for the revival was a scholarly Irish gentleman named Standish O'Grady, who rediscovered in the Royal Irish Society the ancient manuscripts that no one except antiquarians read any more. Dipping into them with all the enthusiasm of an explorer in an inviting unknown land, O'Grady used the tales as source material for a popular history of Ireland in which the Fir Bolgs, Fomoiri and Milesians became characters in what amounted to an Irish version of the Books of Genesis and Exodus in the Old Testament; the great hero Cúchulainn became rather like an Irish Moses.

The members of the Irish literary revival drew upon O'Grady's work in many ways. Lady Gregory recounted the boisterous adventures of Cúchulainn in the form of a collection of decorous Victorian folk

A memorial to an early Celtic priest, this stone slab was placed on a mountainside in southern Ireland around the end of the Fourth Century A.D. Below a Greek cross, the newly converted Christians etched two swastikas—traditional symbols of divine power that date back to prehistoric times —as a precaution against offending the ancient pagan gods. The notches and slashes carved along the edges of the slab form an inscription in ogam, an early Irish script.

tales. In the Abbey Theater, founded by Yeats to foster and promote a new Irish drama, the heroic tales provided the themes for plays conceived to inspire modern Irish audiences.

In a play by the Irish visionary poet George Russell —most commonly known just by the initials A.E.— the name of the great Cúchulainn was uttered on the Irish stage for the first time in history in 1902, thrilling the theater's patriotic audience. After that Cúchulainn dominated many of the Abbey plays, along with King Conchobar and Queen Medb—better known to the Abbey playgoers as Queen Maeve. Yeats himself wrote a total of five Cúchulainn plays; the first of them, *On Bailes Strand,* in 1901; the last, *The Death of Cuchulain,* in 1938.

The Irish literary revival, which got its first impetus as a movement intended to arouse Ireland's pride in the heroic Celtic past, inevitably lead Irish nationalists to use the legends for political purposes as well. The brave Cúchulainn, who had lived so intensely and died as a youth while fighting for high ideals, in time became a symbolic figure for the Irish independence movement that reached its climax in the 1916 Easter Rebellion.

In fact one of the leaders of the rebellion made Cúchulainn his patron saint. His name was Padraic Pearse, an idealistic schoolmaster and a former member of the Gaelic League—an organization devoted to the restoration of Irish as a written and spoken language. Pearse founded a school for boys where Gaelic was taught and the image of Cúchulainn was constantly invoked. A mural of the Celtic warrior confronted every pupil at the school entrance and the boys were urged to emulate his bravery and courage. In the words of one biographer, Pearse wanted

A Heritage in Metalwork

Although the La Tène style of Celtic art, with its whorling designs and dazzling colors, had long since given way in most of Europe to the subdued and literal style of the Romans, the Celtic spirit remained very much alive in the seclusion of Christian Ireland. There, as late as 800 A.D., metalsmiths were combining the new technique of plying fine wires into filigree patterns with the ancient ways of working glass. In the process they created masterpieces directly descended from works produced in Celtic Gaul 10 centuries before. The medieval Irish artists applied their consummate skill to create objects for both secular and sacred uses. Ornaments for a layman's cloak were as sumptuous as those serving in the worship of God.

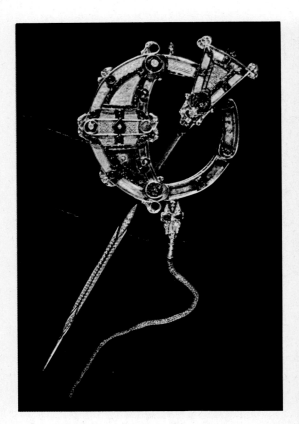

Wrought around 700 A.D. of bronze and silver and decorated with gold filigree, the Tara brooch—named for an ancient Irish city—is equally elegant both on its front (above), which is studded with amber, and on its back (right). Only three inches in diameter, the ring part of the brooch was fastened to the shoulder of a nobleman's woolen cloak by the shaft of a long triangle-topped pin. The snakelike silver chain may have served to attach this brooch to another, similar ornament.

One of Ireland's most treasured masterpieces, the silver Ardagh chalice —only seven inches high—was made in the Eighth Century for the communion service. The sacramental wine was drunk from the golden rim of the cup.

The exquisite craftsmanship of both handles of the Ardagh chalice and the escutcheons below them is clearly visible in this detail. Into the space of only a few inches, the artist worked bands and studs of blue and red enamel and delicate interlaces of gold wire edged with minute granules of gold.

to see an Ireland teeming with Cúchulainns. Like his ancient hero, Padraic Pearse died a martyr to an ideal: he was executed by a British firing squad for his leadership of the rebellion.

But if ancient Irish literature could light up the Celtic past so vividly for men like William Butler Yeats and Padraic Pearse, that same Celtic past could also be newly appreciated in other, less volatile ways by scholars and archeologists. The tangible relics of that past still haunt the highways and byways of the Irish countryside.

Carvings of disembodied human heads appear among the stones in the walls of Irish houses and Christian chapels. On the frieze at the base of a stone cross erected at Ahenny during the Eighth Century, mourners move alongside a funeral procession watched over by pagan vultures, and cowled monks precede a decapitated corpse carried by a donkey.

Today the heritage of the ancient Celts, so proudly claimed by the members of the Irish revival, is at last being examined and studied in a way that is long overdue. History—not only ancient chronicles but modern history as well—has not always dealt kindly with the Celts. Western civilization has tended to emphasize the enormous debt it owes to the civilizations of Greece and Rome, while at the same time it has almost ignored its Celtic inheritance. Yet the Celts, with their feudal societies, their innovative use of iron, their heroic exploits—and most important, the art, literature and scholarship they left—contributed impressively to shaping and enriching much of what is best in the modern world. And at last, in the 20th Century, the legacy of the Celts, with all its varied elements, is receiving the recognition it deserves.

Sanctuaries for Penance and Prayer

The Celts of pagan Ireland, although quick to battle among themselves, succumbed peacefully to Christianity in the Fifth Century A.D. Before long they had cast the new ecclesiastical establishment in the mold of a society long accustomed to tribal rule. Unlike branches of the Church elsewhere in Europe, centrally administered from Rome, the Irish Church took the form of many scattered monasteries, each independently governed by its abbot.

Some of these religious settlements, like those at Glendalough and Clonmacnois, eventually attained enormous wealth and renown as centers of learning, and grew to considerable size. But most were indistinguishable from the humble farmsteads of pre-Christian Ireland—enclosures made of stone or earth encircling a small chapel, with a cluster of huts for the monks' living quarters. Still more ascetic were the communities of monks who, as one monk put it, sought "a solitude in the pathless sea," living hermit-like on the barren, rocky islands that lie off the Irish coast.

Measuring only a trifle over 10 by 15 feet on the inside, this tiny stone chapel marks the location of a former monastic community in County Kerry. It is called the Gallarus Oratory, and it may date from the Eighth Century A.D. Probably it was patterned after wooden or wattle-and-daub churches of even greater antiquity.

A Lonely Outpost of Christian Faith

Seeking spiritual perfection in isolation, one group of Irish monks risked the open sea to settle on the tiny island of Great Skellig, a jagged mass of rock eight miles off the southwestern Irish coast. There, in the early Ninth Century, they established Skellig Michael, a cluster of beehive huts and two small churches clinging to a rocky shelf, 600 feet above the crashing waves of the Atlantic. Lacking trees for lumber, the monks constructed their community of stone, and built stone retaining walls to hold precious pockets of the island's thin soil for gardening.

Weather-beaten and encrusted with lichen, the vaguely cross-shaped stone slab at right still bears the rough carving of a Latin cross. Like similar slabs scattered throughout the island, it may mark the grave of an early monk. Nearby stands one of Skellig Michael's two churches, or oratories, while in the distance lies the islet of Little Skellig, so rocky and barren that the only living creatures it is able to support are colonies of sea birds.

Rounded outside, square inside, Skellig Michael's beehive huts were built with walls as thick as six feet to withstand the blasts of fierce Atlantic gales. Though constructed without mortar and abandoned since the 12th Century, when the monks left the island retreat for the mainland, the shelters have weathered time and the elements in almost perfect condition.

A Thriving Enclave in a Valley

The monastic settlement of Glendalough, enfolded by a narrow, wooded valley with placid lakes about 30 miles south of present-day Dublin, provides a striking contrast to bleak, remote Skellig Michael. Founded in the Sixth Century by St. Kevin, a hermit whose reputation for holiness soon attracted a multitude of followers, Glendalough grew to be one of the largest religious centers in early Christian Ireland. Its fame as a seat of learning drew scholars not only from Ireland and Britain but also from Continental Europe. In time its wealth became so great that it was plundered repeatedly by Vikings. But each time it recovered and continued to flourish until, in the 14th Century, it finally fell into decay.

Glendalough's ruins are scattered along almost two miles of the valley. They range from the simple cave, where tradition says St. Kevin lived as a hermit, to a round bell tower of stone more than 100 feet high.

The best preserved among Glendalough's numerous stone churches is the one seen here, partially hidden behind its sacristy. Known as St. Kevin's Kitchen because the church belfry resembles a chimney, it probably dates from the Ninth Century.

Walled and roofed entirely in stone, St. Kevin's Kitchen was so sturdily designed that for a while in the 19th Century, 800 years after it was built, it was put into use as a church for the valley's community. Its steeply pitched roof, resting on walls nearly four feet thick, is constructed of overlapping layers of stones sealed with mortar. The slant of the roof and the stones' beveled edges shed rain so well that even today the church is still virtually watertight.

The ruins of the church on the spot where St. Ciaran is believed to have died stand swathed in Irish mist. Pilgrims still come to Clonmacnois to scoop up earth in the church's northeast corner, the supposed site of the founder's grave. Dimly seen in the background are the remains of a belfry used as a fort in time of war.

A Holy City on the River Shannon

On the east bank of the River Shannon, near the heart of Ireland, St. Ciaran and a few followers built a small church in the year 548 A.D. From this modest start there arose the monastic complex of Clonmacnois, the burial place of many Irish kings and a rich treasury of medieval Celtic art and literature. Between the Eighth and the 13th centuries, it contained a dozen or more churches, scores of dwellings for monks and armed retainers, and workshops for artisans and scribes. Reduced to ruin before the 16th Century, Clonmacnois still preserves traces of its artistic heyday in its intricately carved stone crosses.

One of several ancient, richly carved stone crosses that are preserved at Clonmacnois, the 10th Century Cross of the Scriptures takes its name from the scenes sculpted on both sides of its shaft. On the front (right) the Crucifixion and the Betrayal of Christ can be seen. In a panel from the other side (left) St. Ciaran and a helper wearing a dagger erect a post for the first church built on the site. The wheel encircling the center of this and many other Irish crosses may trace its ancestry to the sun symbol of the pagan Celts.

Little remains of the Celtic Church in Ireland besides silent ruins like the remnants of Clonmacnois, here silhouetted with its stone crosses against the sky at sundown. Most of the structures of early Christian Ireland—its solitary monasteries and its once wealthy and learned communities—perished in Viking raids or later, when warring Irish factions, Norman conquerors or English armies plundered and destroyed them.

The Emergence of Man

This chart records the progression of life on earth from its first appearance in the warm waters of the new-formed planet through the evolution of man himself; it traces his physical, social, technological and intellectual development to the Christian era. To place these advances in commonly used chronological sequences, the column at the

Geology	Archeology	Billions of Years Ago	
Precambrian earliest era		4.5	Creation of the Earth
		4	Formation of the primordial sea
			First life, single-celled algae and bacteria, appears in water
		3	
		2	
		1	
		Millions of Years Ago	
			First oxygen-breathing animals appear
		800	
			Primitive organisms develop interdependent specialized cells
		600	Shell-bearing multicelled invertebrate animals appear
			Evolution of armored fish, first animals to possess backbones
Paleozoic ancient life		400	Small amphibians venture onto land
			Reptiles and insects arise
			Thecodont, ancestor of dinosaurs, arises
		200	Age of dinosaurs begins
Mesozoic middle life			Birds appear
			Mammals live in shadow of dinosaurs
			Age of dinosaurs ends
		80	
			Prosimians, earliest primates, develop in trees
Cenozoic recent life		60	
		40	Monkeys and apes evolve
		20	
		10	Ramapithecus, oldest known primate with apparently manlike traits, evolves in India and Africa
		8	
		6	Australopithecus, closest primate ancestor to man, appears in Africa
		4	

Geology	Archeology	Millions of Years Ago	
Lower Pleistocene oldest period of most recent epoch	**Lower Paleolithic** oldest period of Old Stone Age	2	Oldest known tool fashioned by man in Africa
		1	First true man, Homo erectus, emerges in East Indies and Africa
			Homo erectus populates temperate zones
		Thousands of Years Ago	
Middle Pleistocene middle period of most recent epoch		800	Man learns to control and use fire
		600	
			Large-scale, organized elephant hunts staged in Europe
		400	Man begins to make artificial shelters from branches
		200	
Upper Pleistocene latest period of most recent epoch	**Middle Paleolithic** middle period of Old Stone Age		Neanderthal man emerges in Europe
		80	
		60	Ritual burials in Europe and Near East suggest belief in afterlife
			Woolly mammoths hunted by Neanderthals in northern Europe
		40	Cave bear becomes focus of cult in Europe
	Upper Paleolithic latest period of Old Stone Age		Cro-Magnon man arises in Europe
			Asian hunters cross Bering Land Bridge to populate New World
			Oldest known written record, lunar notations on bone, made in Europe
			Man reaches Australia
			First artists decorate walls and ceilings of caves in France and Spain
		30	Figurines sculpted for nature worship
		20	Invention of needle makes sewing possible
			Bison hunting begins on Great Plains of North America
Holocene present epoch	**Mesolithic** Middle Stone Age	10	Bow and arrow invented in Europe
			Pottery first made in Japan

(Last Ice Age)

▼ Four billion years ago

▼ Three billion years ago

▲ Origin of the Earth (4.5 billion)

▼ First life (3.5 billion)

ar left of each of the chart's four sections identifies the great geological eras into which the earth's history is divided by scientists, while the second column lists the archeological ages of human history. The key dates in the rise of life and of man's outstanding accomplishments appear in the third column (years and events mentioned in this volume of The Emergence of Man appear in bold type). The chart is not to scale; the reason is made clear by the bar below, which represents in linear scale the 4.5 billion years spanned by the chart—on the scaled bar, the portion relating to the total period of known human existence (far right) is too small to be distinguished.

Geology	Archeology	Years B.C.	
Holocene (cont.)	**Neolithic** New Stone Age	9000	
			Sheep domesticated in Near East
			Dog domesticated in North America
		8000	Jericho, oldest known city, settled
			Goat domesticated in Persia
			Man cultivates his first crops, wheat and barley, in Near East
		7000	Pattern of village life grows in Near East
			Catal Hüyük, in what is now Turkey, becomes largest Neolithic city
			Loom invented in Near East
			Cattle domesticated in Near East
		6000	Agriculture begins to replace hunting in Europe
			Copper used in trade in Mediterranean area
	Copper Age		Corn cultivated in Mexico
		4800	Oldest known massive stone monument built in Brittany
		4000	Sail-propelled boats used in Egypt
			First city-states develop in Sumer
			Cylinder seals begin to be used as marks of identification in Near East
		3500	First potatoes grown in South America
			Wheel originates in Sumer
			Man begins to cultivate rice in Far East
			Silk moth domesticated in China
			Horse domesticated in south Russia
			Egyptian merchant trading ships start to ply the Mediterranean
			Pictographic writing invented in Near East
	Bronze Age	3000	Bronze first used to make tools in Near East
			City life spreads to Nile Valley
			Plow is developed in Near East
			Accurate calendar based on stellar observation devised in Egypt
		2800	Stonehenge, most famous of ancient stone monuments, begun in England
			Pyramids built in Egypt
		2600	Variety of gods and heroes glorified in Gilgamesh and other epics in Near East

Geology	Archeology	Years B.C.	
Holocene (cont.)	**Bronze Age** (cont.)	2500	Cities rise in the Indus Valley
			Earliest evidence of use of skis in Scandinavia
			Earliest written code of laws drawn up in Sumer
			Minoan palace societies begin on Crete
		2000	
			Use of bronze in Europe
			Chicken and elephant domesticated in Indus Valley
			Eskimo culture begins in Bering Strait area
		1500	Invention of ocean-going outrigger canoes enables man to reach islands of South Pacific
			Ceremonial bronze sculptures created in China
			Imperial government, ruling distant provinces, established by Hittites
		1400	Iron in use in Near East
			First complete alphabet devised in script of the Ugarit people in Syria
			Hebrews introduce concept of monotheism
	Iron Age	1000	Reindeer domesticated in Eurasia
			Phoenicians spread alphabet
		900	
		800	**Use of iron begins to spread throughout Europe**
			First highway system built in Assyria
			Homer composes Iliad and Odyssey
			Mounted nomads appear in the Near East as a new and powerful force
		700	Rome founded
			Wheel barrow invented in China
		200	Epics about India's gods and heroes, the Mahabharata and Ramayana, written
			Water wheel invented in Near East
		0	Christian era begins

▼ Two billion years ago

▼ One billion years ago

First oxygen-breathing animals (900 million) ▲

First animals to possess backbones (470 million) ▲

First men (1.3 million) ▲

Acknowledgments

For the help given in the preparation of this book, the editors are particularly indebted to the following people and institutions: Roger Agache, Director of Prehistoric Antiquities, Nord-Picardie Region, Abbeville, France; Wilhelm Angeli, Director, Museum of Natural History, Vienna; Simone Bourland-Collin, Curator, Borély Museum, Marseille, France; R.L.S. Bruce-Mitford, Keeper, Department of Medieval and Later Antiquities, British Museum, London; Bernard Chertier, Director of Prehistoric Antiquities, Champagne-Ardennes Region, Châlons-sur-Marne, France; Georges de Loye, Chief Curator, Calvet Museum, Avignon, France; Simone-Antoinette Deyts, Curator, Museum of Archeology, Dijon, France; Brigid Dolan, Librarian, Royal Irish Academy, Dublin; Lain Duval, Curator, National Museum of Antiquities, Saint-Germain-en-Laye, France; Christiane Eluère, National Museum of Antiquities, Saint-Germain-en-Laye, France; Egon Gersbach, Institute of Prehistory, Tübingen University, Tübingen, Germany; Claireve Grandjouan, Associate Professor of Classics, Hunter College, New York City; Raymond Grosset, Rapho Guillumette, Paris; Franz Hampl, Curator, Lower Austrian Provincial Museum, Vienna; Peter Harbison, Archaeological Advisor, Department of National Monuments, Irish Tourist Board, Dublin; René Joffroy, Chief Curator, National Museum of Antiquities, Saint-Germain-en-Laye, France; Wolfgang Kimmig, Director, Institute of Prehistory, Tübingen University, Tübingen, Germany; Irene Kircher, Photo Archives, German Archeological Institute, Rome; Alfons Kolling, Director, State Museum of Prehistory, Saarbrücken, Germany; Victor Lassalle, Curator, Museum of Art and History, Nîmes, France; A. T. Lucas, Director, The National Museum of Ireland, Dublin; Louis Malbos, Curator, Granet Museum, Aix-en-Provence, France; Günter Mansfeld, Institute of Prehistory, Tübingen University, Tübingen, Germany; Christiane Marandet, Curator, Museums of Besançon, France; J.V.S. Megaw, Professor, Department of Archaeology, University of Leicester, England; Herbert Melichar, Museum of Natural History, Vienna; Marie Montembault, Department of Greek and Roman Antiquities, Louvre Museum, Paris; Mario Monti, Photo Archives, German Archeological Institute, Rome; Friedrich Mossleitner, Engineer, Museum Carolino Augusteum, Salzburg, Austria; David Ojalvo, Curator, Museum of History, Orléans, France; William O'Sulli-

van, Keeper of Manuscripts, Trinity College Library, Dublin; Gaetano Panazza, Director, Civic Museums, Brescia, Italy; Ernst Penninger, Engineer, Celtic Museum, Hallein, Austria; I.J.M. Phillips, Department of Prehistoric and Romano-British Antiquities, British Museum, London; François Salviat, Director of Prehistoric Antiquities, Provence Region, Aix-en-Provence, France; Walter Schaehle, State Museum of Prehistory, Saarbrücken, Germany; Hilmar Schickler, Department of Prehistory, Württemberg State Museum, Stuttgart, Germany; Rudolf Zahler, Hallstatt Museum, Hallstatt, Austria.

The editors would also like to acknowledge permission granted by Kenneth Hurlston Jackson to reprint on page 23 of The Celts an excerpt from his translation of "Edaín the Fairy," published in A Celtic Miscellany in 1967 by Routledge & Kegan Paul. Permission was also given by the Government of Ireland to reprint the poetry found on pages 138 and 140. Translated by James Carney, these poems appear in Early Irish Literature, by Eleanor Knott and Gerard Murphy, published by Barnes & Noble.

Bibliography

General: History and Archeology

Bieler, Ludwig, Ireland: Harbinger of the Middle Ages. Oxford University Press, 1963.

Boardman, John, M. A. Brown, and T.G.E. Powell, eds., The European Community in Later Prehistory. Routledge & Kegan Paul, 1971.

Bowen, E. G., Saints, Seaways and Settlements in the Celtic Islands. University of Wales Press, 1969.

Brogan, Olwen, Roman Gaul. Harvard University Press, 1953.

Caesar, Julius, The Gallic War. Translated by H. J. Edwards. Harvard University Press, 1966.

Chadwick, Nora, The Celts. Penguin Books, 1970.

Clark, J.G.D., Prehistoric Europe. Stanford University Press, 1952.

Collingwood, R. G., and J.N.L. Myres, Roman Britain and the English Settlements. Oxford University Press, 1949.

Cunliffe, Barry, Iron Age Communities in Britain. Routledge & Kegan Paul, 1974.

Dillon, Myles, ed., Early Irish Society. Mercier Press, 1969.

Dillon, Myles, and Nora Chadwick, The Celtic Realms. New American Library, 1967.

Dyer, James, Southern England: An Archaeological Guide. Noyes Press, 1973.

Evans, Estyn, Prehistoric and Early Christian Ireland. Barnes & Noble, 1966.

Filip, Jan, Celtic Civilization and Its Heritage. New Horizons, 1962.

Forbes, R. J., Studies In Ancient Technology, Vol. III. E. J. Brill, 1955.

Fox, Sir Cyril, A Find of the Early Iron Age from Llyn Cerrig Bach, Anglesey. National Museum of Wales, 1946.

Fuller, J.F.C., Julius Caesar: Man, Soldier, and Tyrant. Eyre & Spottiswoode, 1965.

Gimbutas, Marija, Bronze Age Cultures in Central and Eastern Europe. Mouton, 1965.

Harding, D. W., The Iron Age in Lowland Britain. Routledge & Kegan Paul, 1974.

Hatt, Jean-Jacques, Celts and Gallo-Romans. Nagel, 1970.

Holmes, T. Rice, Caesar's Conquest of Gaul. Oxford University Press, 1911.

Hubert, Henri:
The Greatness and Decline of the Celts. Benjamin Blom, 1972.

The Rise of the Celts. Biblo and Tannen, 1966.

Jackson, Kenneth H., The Oldest Irish Tradition: A Window on the Iron Age. Cambridge University Press, 1964.

Kenney, James F., Sources for the Early History of Ireland. Octagon, 1966.

Livy, The Early History of Rome. Translated by Aubrey de Selincourt. Penguin Books, 1973.

MacGearailt, Gearoid, Celts and Normans. Gill and Macmillan, 1969.

McNally, Robert, Old Ireland. Fordham University Press, 1965.

Moody, T. W., and F. X. Martin, The Course of Irish History. Weybright and Talley, 1967.

Norman, E. R., and J.K.S. St. Joseph, The Early Development of Irish Society: The Evidence of Aerial Photography. Cambridge University Press, 1969.

Pausanias, Guide to Greece, Vol. I. Translated by Peter Levi. Penguin Books, 1971.

Piggott, Stuart, Ancient Europe. Aldine Press, 1965.

Polybius, Histories. Translated by W. R. Paton. Harvard University Press, 1922.

Powell, T.G.E., The Celts. Praeger, 1958.

Raftery, Joseph, ed., The Celts. Mercier Press, 1967.

Richmond, I. A., Roman Britain. Barnes & Noble, 1964.

Ross, Anne, Everyday Life of the Pagan Celts. Putnam, 1970.

Singer, Charles, E. J. Holmyard, and A. R. Hall, eds., A History of Technology, Vol. I. Oxford University Press, 1967.

Tierney, J. J., "The Celtic Ethnography of Posidonius," Proceedings of The Royal Irish Academy, 1960.

Vlahos, Olivia, The Battle-Ax People. Viking, 1968.

Wheeler, R.E.M., Maiden Castle Dorset. Oxford University Press, 1943.

Wightman, Edith Mary, Roman Trier and the Treveri. Hart-Davis, 1970.

Literature and Art

Cross, Tom Peete, and Clark Harris Slover, eds., Ancient Irish Tales. Barnes & Noble, 1969.

Finlay, Ian, Celtic Art: An Introduction. Noyes Press, 1973.

Fox, Sir Cyril, Pattern and Purpose: A Survey of Early Celtic Art in Britain. National Museum of Wales, 1958.

Henry, Françoise:
Irish Art in the Early Christian Period. Methuen, 1940.
Irish Art in the Early Christian Period to 800 A.D. Methuen, 1965.
Irish Art during the Viking Invasions. Methuen, 1967.

Hoagland, Kathleen, 1000 Years of Irish Poetry. Devin-Adair, 1947.

Jackson, Kenneth H., trans., A Celtic Miscellany. Routledge & Kegan Paul, 1967.

Jacobsthal, Paul, Early Celtic Art, Vols. I and II. Clarendon Press, 1964.

Kinsella, Thomas, trans., The Tain. Oxford University Press, 1972.

Knott, Eleanor, and Gerard Murphy, Early Irish Literature. Barnes & Noble, 1966.

Laistner, M.L.W., Thought and Letters of Western Europe. Cornell University Press, 1957.

Lucas, A. T., Treasures of Ireland. Viking, 1973.

MacCana, Proinsias, Celtic Mythology. Hamlyn, 1973.

Megaw, J.V.S., Art of the European Iron Age. Harper & Row, 1970.

Pobé, Marcel, and Jean Roubier, The Art of Roman Gaul. Gallery Press, 1961.

Powell, T.G.E., Prehistoric Art. Praeger, 1966.

Rees, Alwyn and Brinley, Celtic Heritage. Thames and Hudson, 1961.

Ross, Anne, Pagan Celtic Britain. Routledge & Kegan Paul, 1967.

Sandars, N. K., Prehistoric Art in Europe. Penguin Books, 1968.

Thompson, William Irwin, The Imagination of an Insurrection. Harper & Row, 1967.

Torbrugge, Walter, Prehistoric European Art. Abrams, 1968.

Religion

Chadwick, Nora K., The Druids. University of Wales Press, 1966.

Clarke, C.P.S., and Rosemary Edisford, Everyman's Book of Saints. Philosophical Library, 1968.

De Paor, Maire and Liam, Early Christian Ireland. Praeger, 1958.

Duke, John A., The Columban Church. Oxford University Press, 1932.

Hughes, Kathleen, Early Christian Ireland. Cornell University Press, 1972.

McNeill, John T., The Celtic Churches. University of Chicago Press, 1974.

Piggott, Stuart, The Druids. Praeger, 1968.

Index

Numerals in italics indicate an illustration of the subject mentioned.